Blue Line 4

Workbook

Herausgeber: Dr. Frank Haß

Ernst Klett Verlag
Stuttgart • Leipzig

Unit 1

Gateway NYC

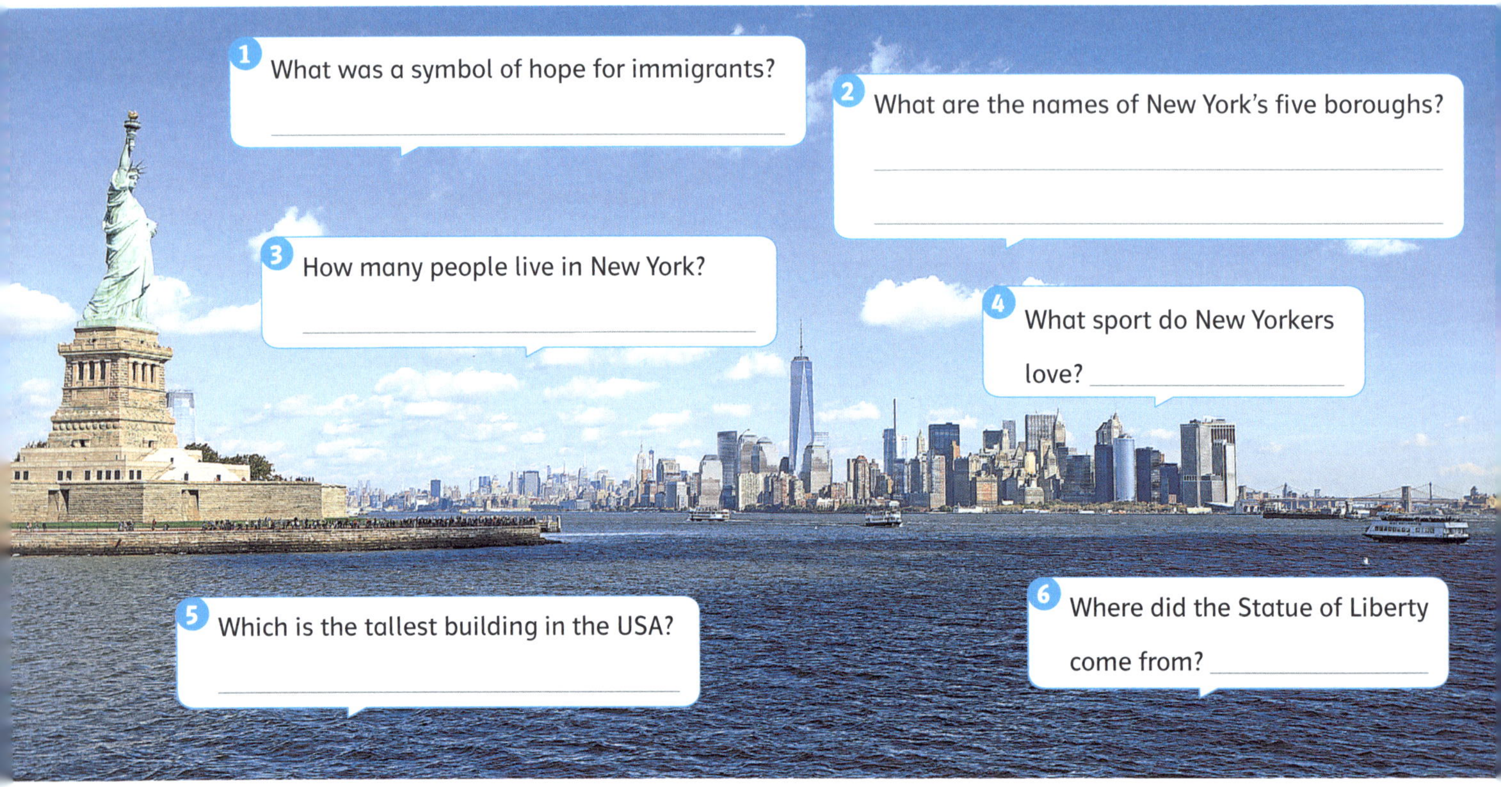

12/2

1 A quiz about New York City

a) Write the answers to the questions in the picture.

b) Find the answers to these questions on the internet.

1. New York got its name in 1664. What was its name before 1664? ______
2. What is the name of the most famous park in Manhattan? ______
3. Which bridge connects Manhattan and Brooklyn? ______

12/2

2 (WRITING) Write sentences about New York. Use these words and numbers.

1. baseball: ______
2. five: ______
3. 8.5 million: ______
4. music: ______
5. 100 years: ______

______

1 Write the words for the pictures.

14/1

1. ______________

2. ______________

3. ______________

4. ______________

5. ______________

6. ______________

7. ______________

8. ______________

2 (LISTENING) Listen to the tour guide. Put a circle around the right answer.

1
15/5

1. Times Square is famous for its skyscrapers • shops • theaters.
2. The theater shows on Broadway are expensive • amazing • boring.
3. The Empire State Building was the tallest building in the world for almost 30 • 40 • 50 years.
4. Fifth Avenue is an expensive shopping street • department store • park.
5. One World Trade Center was built after the attacks on September 11, 2001 • 2007 • 2011.
6. Wall Street is a shopping • tourist • financial center.

3 A New Yorker talks to a tourist

5/5a)

a) Complete these sentences with one or two words.

1. ______________ you can see the Empire State Building.
2. Don't ______________ Times Square, and right ______________ is Central Park.
3. Around ______________ we'll come to the One World Trade Center.
4. You must ______________ Broadway.

5/5b)

b) Complete these sentences with more than one word.

1. Have a look ______________________________
2. In the distance ______________________________
3. From here ______________________________
4. Make sure ______________________________

4 Complete the sentences in the simple past.

16/6

1. From 1785 to 1790 New York _was_ ______ the capital of the USA. (be)
2. The British people ______________ New York its name. (give)
3. Many immigrants ______________ English when they arrived in New York. (not speak)
4. The zoo in Central Park ______________ with a few animals in cages. (start)
5. One World Trade Center ______________ in 2014. (open)
6. It ______________ the Old World Trade Center after the attacks in 2001. (replace)
7. A lot of public transport ______________ in October 2012 because of bad weather. (not work)

5 Write sentences in the simple past.

16/7a)

a) Last weekend Henry stayed in New York. Look at his list and write what he did there.

see a Broadway show	visit One World Trade Center
eat a hot dog	take photos of Times Square
buy some souvenirs	run in Central Park
go to a baseball game	

1. Scott _saw a Broadway show_ ______________ .
2. He ______________ .
3. ______________ .
4. ______________ .
5. ______________ .
6. ______________ .
7. ______________ .

16/7b)

b) What did you do on your last holiday? Write five sentences in your exercise book.

6 Back at home Henry is talking to a friend. Complete the questions and answers.

17/8a)

1. _Did_ you _like_ your trip to New York? (like) – Yes, _I did_ .
2. ______ you ______ in a hotel? (stay) – No, ______ .
3. ______ you ______ lots of American food? (eat) – Yes, ______ .
4. ______ you ______ any TV or movie stars? (see) – No, ______ .
5. ______ you ______ to any museums? (go) – No, ______ .
6. ______ you ______ a baseball shirt? (buy) – Yes, ______ .
7. ______ you ______ the Empire State Building? (visit) – No, ______ .

17/8a)

7 Write questions and answers in the simple past.

1. when / go to New York? • go last weekend

   When did you go to New York ? I went last weekend.

2. what food / eat? • eat hot dogs

   ? .

3. what Broadway show / see? • see Cats

   ? .

4. what building / visit? • visit One World Trade Center

   ? .

5. why / not go to any museums? • not have time

   ? .

6. where / take this photo? • take in Central Park

   ? .

17/8b)

8 (WRITING) Ask your partner.

a) Write six questions for your partner about a city he / she visited.

visit city | see sights | go to restaurants
eat food | see shows | use public transport
visit museums | stay in hotel | ...

1. Which city did you visit?
2.
3.
4.
5.
6.

b) Write your partner's answers.

1. He / She visited.
2.
3.
4.
5.
6.

1 Complete the sentences with the words.

18/1

1. The Cubans in America take their work ________________ .
2. Cuba is a ____________ country.
3. Some Cubans make the ______________ to move to the USA.
4. José is a very ________________ person.
5. They often live in a _________________ with other Cubans.
6. They are ________________ and work hard.

community | decision | successful | poor | motivated | seriously

2 Match the sentences.

19/4a)

1. I would like to emigrate
2. Many people immigrate
3. In my town I have many
4. It doesn't take a long time to
5. When you go to Africa, everything feels

a) get used to foreign food.
b) opportunities to get a good job.
c) from my country.
d) foreign.
e) to another country.

3 Underline the right word.

19/4b)

1. If I learn a lot, I will succeed in • on life.
2. I hope I get support by • from my parents.
3. I'm sure I won't fail on • at work today.
4. I hope I have the right • true papers.

4 (LISTENING) Listen to Angela's friend Kirstie. Take notes ...

2
19/4

1. about how Kirstie met Angela: On Angela's first day at school,
2. about how Kirstie helped Angela (2 things):
3. about the problems Angela had in the US (2 things):

5 Put in the past perfect.

20/6

1. I had watched a lot of movies about America before I went there. (watch)
2. I ______ a foreign country before I came here. (not visit)
3. After we ______ in New York, my dad met us at the bus station. (arrive)
4. I was very excited because I ______ in a big city like this before. (not live)
5. My mom couldn't find at job because she ______ English. (not learn)
6. After my parents ______ their own shop, life became easier for us. (open)

6 Complete the table.

20/6

infinitive	simple past	past participle
leave	left	left
		met
	went	
lose		
		made
	saw	
take		
		eaten

Eine Liste der unregelmäßigen Verben findest du in deinem Buch auf Seite 216.

7 Complete Angela's sentences with the past perfect.

20/6

1. After my plane had left (leave) the Philippines, I started to feel excited about my new life.
2. I ______ (not meet) my aunt and uncle before I went to live with them.
3. After I ______ (move) to the USA, I missed my parents a lot.
4. Before I went to America, I ______ (not see) snow in the winter.
5. I found it hard to make friends before I ______ (learn) English.
6. After my uncle ______ (work) hard for many years, he lost his job.
7. After my uncle ______ (lose) his job, I had to find a student job to make money.
8. After I ______ (finish) school, I stayed friends with Kirstie.

8 Read what Angela did yesterday and put in the simple past or past perfect.

20/7a)

eat breakfast ✓ → go to gymnasium ✓ → finish her training → drink some water
→ take a shower → put on her clothes → pack her bag → call her friends
→ talk to her friends → leave the gymnasium → meet her friends → go to restaurant
→ order their meals → look at the menu

1. After Angela *had eaten* breakfast, she *went* to the gymnasium.
2. After she ____________ her training, she ____________ some water.
3. After she ____________ a shower, she ____________ on her clothes.
4. Before she ____________ her bag, she ____________ her friends.
5. After she ____________ to her friends, she ____________ the gymnasium.
6. After she ____________ her friends, they ____________ to a restaurant together.
7. Before they ____________ their meals, they ____________ at the menu.

9 Write four things you did yesterday and make sentences with the past perfect.

20/7b)

____________ → ____________ → ____________ → ____________

1. *After I had* ____________
2. *After I* ____________

10 Write questions and answers with the past perfect and simple past.

21/8a)

1. meet Angela • before she come to school?
   Had you met Angela before she came to school? – No, *I hadn't*.
2. show someone around • before you help Angela?
   ____________ – Yes, ____________.
3. meet people fromt Philippines • before you meet Angela?
   ____
   – No, ____________.
4. try to speak another language • before Angela become your friend?
   ____
   – Yes, ____________.
5. Angela see snow • before she spend her first winter in the USA?
   ____
   – No, ____________.

21/9

1 (YOUR TURN) Where would you like to go?

You are in New York City with your class.
Look at the brochure. Where would you like to go? Where wouldn't you like to go? Why / why not?
Talk to your group and decide where you want to go together.

- I would go to … because I like …
- I wouldn't go to … because I don't like …
- I think the … sounds interesting / exciting because …
- The … sounds boring …
- …

Central Park
Ride the boats; visit the Central Park Zoo; have a picnic; go swimming in the Lasker Pool; go running or walking around the park; go to a café

Rockefeller Center
See the view from the top; go to the shops and restaurants; see the famous Christmas tree (in winter); go to the computer game center or TV studio

Times Square
See the lights and colors; go shopping or to restaurants; go to Madame Tussauds Museum; watch a movie and eat popcorn

One World Trade Center
See the great view at the top; go to the September 11 Museum; go to the restaurant at the top; go shopping

1 (READING) Read the story.

23/5

My name is Iona O'Brian. I was born in a small village on the west coast of Ireland in 1928. We were a poor family, so my dad emigrated to the USA when I was just five. My mum, little brother and I wanted to follow him there, but it took him nine years to save enough money for our voyage. One day my mum got a letter from my dad with three tickets to America. We were so happy to start a new life and to see our dad again but also sad to leave our home and all our friends and family. The trip on the ship was horrible. It took over a week and we were all sick. We were so happy when we finally arrived in New York City and saw the Statue of Liberty!

Dad was there to meet us. We got on a bus with all our bags and went past the biggest buildings I had ever seen. So many people and cars! We arrived at a street of houses with a big bridge behind them. Dad told us that was the Manhattan Bridge. Mum was happy because the houses looked clean. But when we went inside, we saw that we had only one room for all of us and one bathroom to share with the other people in the house. Mum and Dad had a big argument and Mum said she wanted to go home. I liked it because everything in New York was new and interesting. There were also kids from lots of other countries on our street, and I soon made friends with some of them.

Dad worked long hours in a factory all week. Mum found a job in a big department store, and my brother and I went to school. But the best part of the week was Saturdays. Every Saturday night my friends and I went to a dance at the church hall. I loved the music!

When I was sixteen, I told my mum I wanted to be a writer. She laughed and said that anything can happen in America. I got a job at a small Irish newspaper in Brooklyn and helped my family to save for our own house. Later I worked for a big national newspaper. I have had so many opportunities in America!

2 Right or wrong? Tick the right box.

23/5

	right	wrong
1. Iona was born in a small village in Ireland.	☐	☐
2. She went to America when she was five.	☐	☐
3. In New York the whole family had to live in one room.	☐	☐
4. Iona liked New York from the beginning.	☐	☐
5. There were immigrants from lots of other countries.	☐	☐
6. Iona didn't have any friends.	☐	☐
7. Iona liked dances and music.	☐	☐
8. Iona got a job at a small Irish newspaper in Queens.	☐	☐

3 Underline the answers in the text. Then answer the questions.

23/5

1. Why did Iona have to wait nine years until she could go to America?

____

2. Did Iona enjoy the voyage to New York? Why / why not?

____

____

3. What jobs did Iona's mum and dad have?

____

____

4. What did Iona do in her free time?

____

5. What job did Iona want to have?

____

4 (WRITING) Write titles for the pictures in the story.

23/5

Use the words in the boxes or your own ideas. Write the titles under the photos.
Example: Photo 1: Iona in Ireland when her dad leaves for America

Iona O'Brian	at the newspaper	her dad leaves	Ireland	street
American school	office	New York City	students	…

INTERNET

Dos and don'ts for the American flag

The American flag is very important to people in the USA. Here are some things to think about if you want to put up an American flag yourself:

- **DO** hang flags so the stars are at the top and on the left.
- **DO** put the US flag on the left if you are also hanging up flags from other countries.
- **DO** put a light on the flag if you hang it up after dark.
- **DON'T** draw or write on top of the flag.
- **DON'T** use the flag as clothes.
- **DON'T** use a dirty or broken flag.

24/2 **1** (MEDIATION) Beantworte die Fragen.

1. Was sollte man beim Aufhängen der amerikanischen Flagge alles beachten?

____

____

____

2. Was darf man nicht mit der amerikanischen Flagge machen?

____

____

____

24/2 **2** Complete the telephone call.

Helpline: Hello. This is the US citizen helpline. What can I do for you today?
You: (sage, dass du Informationen möchtest, wie man die US Staatsbürgerschaft bekommt)

____

Helpline: OK. We have tips on our website which you can download.
You: (frage, ob man einen Test machen muss)

Thanks. _______________

Helpline: Yes, first you have to take an English test and then there is a test about the US government and American history.
You: (sage, dass das schwierig klingt und frage, wie man sich darauf vorbereiten kann)

____

Helpline: There is lots of learning material which you can also download.
You: (bedanke dich für die Hilfe)

____

1. Löse alle Aufgaben.
2. Überprüfe deine Lösungen online. Gib dazu den 🌐-Code (nach Ziel 5) auf www.klett.de ein.
3. Gib dir selbst Punkte. Wenn du weniger als die Hälfte der Punkte hast, male das Kästchen rot aus und übe auf den Step by step-Seiten (z. B. bei Unit 1 auf S. 16 – 17).

Ziel 1: Ich kann Informationen über New York verstehen.

New York City is the largest city in the USA with about 8.5 million inhabitants. It is on the Northeast Coast, on the Atlantic Ocean. New York has five boroughs: The Bronx, Brooklyn, Queens, Manhattan and Staten Island. New York is famous for its tall skyscrapers. It has many famous tourist sights which visitors from around the world come to see, for example One World Trade Center, the Empire State Building and Times Square. New York is the financial center of the world but it is also an important place for culture like modern art, theater and music. The most famous symbol of New York is the Statue of Liberty. It celebrates the independence of the US.

Answer the questions.

1. How many people live in New York City? ______
2. How many boroughs does the city have? ______
3. What type of culture can you find in New York? ______
4. What sights can you see in New York? ______
5. Why is the Statue of Liberty New York's most famous symbol? ______

5P

→ p. 16/1

Ziel 2: Ich kann interessante Orte einer Stadt präsentieren.

Look at the information and write a short text about the Empire State Building.

Empire State Building

built:	in 1931
where:	Manhattan
height:	102 stories, 443 metres tall (was the tallest building in the world until 1970)
inside:	shops and offices, great view of Manhattan from the top of the building
visitors:	about 3.5 million every year

______

7P

→ p. 16/2

Ziel 3: Ich kann einen Artikel über eine Person schreiben.

Interviewer: Hi Dolores! You're an immigrant from Mexico. Tell us more about that.
Dolores: Hi! Yes, I was born in Mexico in 1999. I emigrated to the US with my parents and my two brothers in 2007.
Interviewer: Why did your family leave Mexico?
Dolores: We left Mexico because we were very poor. My dad did not have a job and my mom sold fruit and vegetables at the local market. My dad had a cousin with a company in the US. My dad got a job at his cousin's company so we moved to the US.
Interviewer: Did you like your new life in America?
Dolores: No, at first I felt very lonely. I didn't have any friends. My English wasn't very good so I was afraid to talk to the other girls at school.
Interviewer: So what did you do?
Dolores: I started to help at an animal rescue shelter after school and there I met Allyson, who is now my best friend. She helped me a lot. Today I'm really happy to be here in the US because there are so many opportunities.

Read the interview and write an article about Dolores.

Dolores was born in Mexico in 1999. She emigrated to the US with her parents and two brothers in 2007.

8P

→ p. 17/3

Ziel 4: Ich kann einen Text über die Geschichte der Einwanderung verstehen.

Read the text on page 10 again. Tick the right box.

	right	wrong
1. Iona's dad emigrated to US when she was five.	☐	☐
2. The trip on the ship was awful.	☐	☐
3. Her mom liked their one room in the new house.	☐	☐
4. Her dad worked a lot in the factory.	☐	☐
5. Her mom did not find a job.	☐	☐
6. On Fridays there were dances at the church hall.	☐	☐
7. Later Iona worked for different newspapers.	☐	☐

7P

→ p. 17/4

Ziel 5: Ich kann Informationen über Einbürgerung weitergeben.

Can you become a US citizen?

Are you 18 or older?
Have you been a permanent resident of the United States (for more than 5 years)?
Are you a person of good moral character?
Do you have a basic knowledge of the US government and history?
Are you able to read, write and speak basic English?

If you want to become a US citizen, come to our information center. We will help you to:

- fill in the forms
- prepare for the English and US history tests
- prepare for the interview.

a) Lies dir den Flyer durch und beantworte die Fragen auf Deutsch.

1. Wie lange muss man in den USA gewohnt haben, bis man die Staatsbürgerschaft beantragen kann?

   ____

2. Wie gut muss man English können? ______________________________
3. Wobei hilft das Informationszentrum? ______________________________

   ____

b) Complete the telephone call.

Helpline: Hello, this is the Information Center. What can I do for you today?
You: (sage, dass du US-Staatsbürger werden möchtest und Hilfe brauchst)

____

Helpline: OK. In our courses we can help you prepare for the tests and for the interview.
You: (frage, wie viel ein Kurs kostet) ______________________________
Helpline: All the courses are free.
You: (sage, dass das toll ist und frage, wann die Kurse sind)

____

Helpline: The courses are every Monday and Wednesday at 7 p.m.
You: (bedanke dich für die Hilfe) ______________________________

7P
→ p. 17/5

Lösungen online
fz43g9

○ Ziel 1: Ich kann Informationen über New York verstehen.

INTERNET ×

Over 54 million tourists visit New York every year. The most popular place for tourists is Times Square because of the signs, restaurants and shops. Many tourists also visit One World Trade Center and Central Park. Other popular sights are the Metropolitan Museum of Art, the Empire State Building and Rockefeller Center. In the evenings the Broadway shows are very popular.

Complete the sentences.

1. Over 54 million tourists visit ______________________________.
2. The most popular place for tourists is ______________________________.
3. Times Square has lots of signs, ______________________________.
4. Many tourists also visit ______________________________.
5. In the evenings the Broadway shows ______________________________.

○ Ziel 2: Ich kann interessante Orte einer Stadt präsentieren.

Look at the information and complete the text about One World Trade Center.

One World Trade Center

built: from 2006 to 2013
where: Manhattan
height: 104 stories, 546 metres tall (the tallest building in the US)
inside: offices and restaurants, great view of Manhattan from the top

One World Trade Center was built ______________
______________ .
______________ in Manhattan.
______________ 104 stories and
is ______________ tall.
______________ the highest building ______________ .
______________ there are offices and restaurants.
You have ______________
______________ of the building.

○ **Ziel 3: Ich kann einen Artikel über eine Person schreiben.**

Read Kim's answers from an interview and complete the text.

Kim Wu comes from ______________________ .

She ________________ in 1996. In 2014

she ____________________________ . Now she

lives ____________________________ .

________________________ are still in China.

Kim is a ______________ . In the evenings she

works ______________________ .

Name? Kim Wu
From? Guangzhou, China
Born? 1996
Immigrated to USA? 2014
Home now? Brooklyn, New York
Family? mom and dad in China
Job? student, job in a restaurant

○ **Ziel 4: Ich kann einen Text über die Geschichte der Einwanderung verstehen.**

Read the text on pages 22–23 in your book again and put the sentences in the right order.

- [ ] At the end of the long trip, many passengers were sick.
- [ ] If the immigrants were too weak to work, the doctors sent them back to their home countries.
- [1] Families often saved money for the father or the oldest son to make the journey.
- [ ] After the ship had arrived in Manhattan, they went to Ellis Island on a small boat.
- [ ] Before they could leave the ship, doctors came on board.
- [ ] The voyage took seven to 21 days.
- [ ] On Ellis Island there were more checks and personal interviews.

○ **Ziel 5: Ich kann Informationen über Einbürgerung weitergeben.**

Lies dir den Flyer durch und beantworte die Fragen auf Deutsch.

Would you like to be a US citizen?

Do you need help with the forms?
Do you need help with your English?
Do you want to prepare for the US history and the government test?

We can help you with your American Dream!

Call us or visit our website!

1. Für wen ist der Flyer?

____

____

2. Wobei bekommt man Hilfe?

____

____

____

____

3. Wie bekommt man mehr Informationen?

____

____

A INTERNET ×

Hamptons

The Hamptons are a group of villages in the towns of Southampton and East Hampton. They are at the end of Long Island, northeast of New York City. When New York gets hot in the summer, many New Yorkers like to escape to the cooler seaside villages and beaches in the area. You can travel to the Hamptons by train, bus or car.
The houses there are some of the most expensive in the US and lots of stars spend their weekends or holidays there. In the summer there are a lot of tourists in the Hamptons because there are lots of good restaurants, shops, farmers' markets and beaches.

B INTERNET ×

What's hot in the Hamptons this summer?

I've found the coolest events for you this weekend!

» Pop-up shops in Southampton
There are some cool new pop-up shops with clothes and swimwear. Look what I bought yesterday!

» Cat Yoga
I've tried the new yoga class which has cats from the animal rescue shelter at YogaSun studio in East Hampton. Everyone says that cats help you to relax and feel happy. All I can say: it's true!

» White Beach Party
At Navy Beach next Saturday from 7 p.m. Food, drinks and live music. Wear white. Hope to see you there!

C INTERNET ×

NEWS | STYLE | RED CARPET | EVENTS | MORE

NEWS

STAR SPOTTED!
Khloé Kardashian out for dinner in a Hampton's restaurant Moby's.

Making films and shows
People are always making films and shows in the Hamptons, so you may see some of the stars of *The Real Housewives of New York City or Revenge*.

31/4 ## 1 Check the information.

Look at the three websites. What kind of websites are they? Look at the tip for help.

1. Website A is ______________________________
   ______________________________ .
2. Website B is ______________________________ .
3. Website C is ______________________________
   ______________________________ .

You should know where the information that you've found comes from. Official websites have a lot of information, for example for tourists. Blogs have people's opinions. An online magazine writes about news, stars, fashion etc.

31/4 ## 2 Find out information.

a) Read the three websites and underline the most important keywords for each website.
b) Write the keywords in the table.

Website A	Website B	Website C
villages	*cool events*	*stars spotted*

31/4 ## 3 Search the internet.

a) What other information would you like to know about the Hamptons? Write down some keywords.

____

____

____

b) Use your keywords and search for information on the internet. List two different websites where you found useful information.

____

____

c) Tell your partner what you found out.

Unit 2

Teens in the Midwest

32/2 3 **1** (LISTENING) **Listen to Elliot talking about his life in the Midwest.**

a) Put the pictures in the right order.

b) Listen again and complete the sentences.

Elliot's ______________ Math test was a disaster.

On the ______________ he works in a restaurant.

It's ______________ at Robinson High School this weekend.

As a kid he was afraid of ______________ .

The school has a ______________ football team.

Native ______________ history makes him sad.

33/3 **2** **Search the internet.**

a) Find the answers to the questions.

1. Which twelve US states belong to the Midwest? ______________
2. Which city in the Midwest has the most inhabitants? ______________
3. What's the name of the deadliest tornado in the US so far? ______________
4. Which Native American is on a $1 coin? ______________

b) Find two more facts about one state in the Midwest.

1. ______________
2. ______________

1 Write school words.

35/4a)

a) Make words. Look at the words (At American schools) on page 190 in your book.

Ma ✓	elec	+	tive	leader
prin	cla		th ✓	ion
detent	morning		ker	cipal
cheer	loc		ss	message

Math, p

b) Write six more words for each heading.

School subjects	School things
Math,	pen,

2 What are the words?

35/4a)

a) Write a word under each picture.

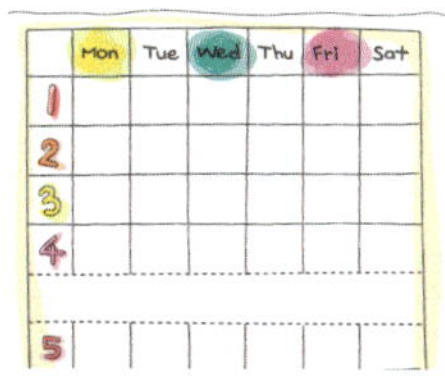

1. ______ 2. ______ 3. ______ 4. ______ 5. ______

35/4b)

b) Write the words for the definitions.

1. Another word for holiday: ______
2. Subjects you can choose are ______
3. The American word for lesson: ______
4. The area and buildings around a school: ______

3 (YOUR TURN) Write about a day at your school.

35/5

Most students go to school by

4 35/5

4 (LISTENING) Listen to Luise and her friend Elliot. Tick the right box.

	right	wrong
1. Luise thinks the Pledge of Allegiance is strange.	☐	☐
2. Luise likes the lockers because they look nice.	☐	☐
3. Elliot once forgot a sandwich in his locker.	☐	☐
4. The sandwich was still good.	☐	☐
5. Luise is now a cheerleader.	☐	☐
6. Luise and Elliot want to go to a restaurant after the football game.	☐	☐

36/7

5 Complete the sentences with was allowed to or wasn't allowed to.

1. Luise *was allowed to choose* her electives. — choose ✓
2. She *was* ______ her homework in study hall. — do ✓
3. She ______ in study hall. — eat ✗
4. She ______ her laptop to school. — bring ✓
5. She ______ things in the classroom. — keep ✗
6. She ______ the cheerleading team. — join ✓
7. She ______ short dresses. — wear ✗

36/8a)

6 Complete Aileen's sentences with was able to or wasn't able to.

- speak English ☺
- choose every elective ☹
- see the Empire State Building ☺
- travel to the West Coast ☹
- find my way ☺
- get a place ☹
- see the Atlantic ☺
- make new friends ☺

1. I *was able to speak English* when I came to the USA.
2. I *was* ______ to my classrooms.
3. I ______ I liked.
4. I ______ on the cheerleading team.
5. I ______ when I visited New York.
6. I ______ when I was in the USA.
7. I ______ because it was too far away.
8. I ______ at my American school.

36/8a)

7 Was (not) able to or was (not) allowed to? Underline the right words.

1. Jannik **was able to** • **was not able to** understand the other students. (+)
2. The students **weren't allowed to** • **were allowed to** wear jeans. (+)
3. Jannik **wasn't able to** • **was able to** read difficult books in English. (–)
4. He **wasn't allowed to** • **was allowed to** use the computers at school. (+)
5. He **was allowed to** • **wasn't allowed to** bring his own laptop to school. (–)
6. He **was able to** • **wasn't able to** help others with their German homework. (+)
7. They **weren't allowed to** • **were allowed to** bring food to the cafeteria. (+)
8. They **were allowed to** • **weren't allowed to** keep food in their lockers. (–)

be able to = Fähigkeit
be allowed to = Erlaubnis

36/8b)

8 What were you allowed to do or (not) allowed to do when you were younger? Write four sentences with I was allowed to or I wasn't allowed to.

have a phone | eat lots of sweets | watch TV | . . .

1. When I was three years old, I wasn't allowed to ______
2. When I was six years old, ______
3. When I ______
4. ______

37/9

9 Make sentences with had to or didn't have to.

a) Look at Luise's teacher's list and complete the sentences.

1. On Monday he had to ______ get up at seven o'clock.
2. He didn't ______ go to Computer Club.
3. He ______ teach a Math class.
4. He ______ organize the class trip.
5. He ______ talk to the principal.
6. He ______ watch the football game.
7. He ______ check his students' homework.
8. He ______ go to bed early.

To do on Monday

get up at seven o'clock
teach a Math class
organize the class trip
check his students' homework
go to bed early

b) What about you? Write three sentences about yesterday.

1. Yesterday I ______
2. ______
3. ______

38/3

1 Put in the right words.

manager | people | ad | wages | interview | apply for | allowance ✓

My mom has always given me an allowance every month. Now it's 40 dollars. I don't think that's very much. So when I saw an ________ in the sports store for a student job, I decided to ________ it. At first I thought the ________ was scary. At my ________ he asked me some difficult questions. But now I think he is cool and so are the other ________ who work there. I work every Saturday and Sunday from 9 a.m. to 5 p.m. I save all my ________ because I want to buy a car.

39/6a)

2 Read Michael's job interview and put in the right words.

responsible | hard-working | lazy ✓ | cooperative | bossy | friendly | unmotivated

1. Do you work hard? – Yes, I'm not lazy. I'm ________.
2. Do you like working with other people? – Yes, I'm ________ and ________.
3. Can you tell people what to do? – Yes, but I am not ________.
4. Do you always arrive at school on time? – Yes, of course. I'm very ________.
5. Do you always do your homework? – No, if my homework is boring, I'm a bit ________.

39/6b)

3 Write the words for these definitions.

1. When you are ________, you give money or presents to other people.
2. When you are ________, you only think about yourself.
3. When you are ________, you don't like meeting new people.
4. When you are ________, you are not polite.
5. The opposite of shy is ________.

5
39/7

4 (LISTENING) Michael talks to his friend Billy. Listen and answer the questions.

1. What is Michael looking for? ______
2. Who does Michael want to impress? ______
3. How does Billy go to people's houses? ______
4. Why is Billy sometimes tired? ______
5. Why did Billy have to stay in an old lady's house? ______
6. What can be dangerous about Billy's job? ______

40/8

5 What does Michael say? Complete the sentences.

1. If you need a smaller size, I 'll find (find) it for you.
2. If you ______ (not leave) the store, I'll call the manager.
3. If you ______ (need) more time to choose, I'll come back later.
4. If you buy two T-shirts, you ______ (get) one free.

5. If you want another color, I ______ (ask) my co-worker.
6. My boss ______ (be) angry if I talk too much to the customers.
7. I ______ (not help) you if you are rude.
8. My co-worker will look for a tennis dress if you ______ (want) one.

40/9a)

6 Read the special offers at Fruit4U and complete the sentences.

1. If you buy (buy) one box of apples, you 'll get (get) a sticker.
2. If you ______ (collect) six stickers, we ______ (give) you a pineapple for free!
3. If you ______ (come) to the store on your birthday, we ______ (sing) to you.
4. You ______ (pay) 10 % less if you ______ (spend) more than 30 dollars.
5. You ______ (find) our fresh fruit salad if you ______ (visit) our store on a Monday.
6. You ______ (get) a box of oranges if you ______ (bring) a new customer to the store.

40/9a)

7 Michael is going to another job interview at a clothes store. What does he think? Write if-clauses.

1. the manager be bossy • not take the job

   If the manager is bossy, ______________________

2. the wages are good • save money for a car

   If ______________________

3. the people there are friendly • make some new friends

   ____

4. the job is boring • look for another job

   ____

5. have to work on a Sunday • say I have baseball practice

   ____

6. the boss like me • ask for more money

   ____

41/10a)

8 Michael is talking to customers at the clothes store. Put in one or ones.

Benutze „ones", um Pluralwörter zu ersetzen.

1. Can I try on some red T-shirts? I don't like the green ones.
2. I need two T-shirts – a red ______ and a blue ______.
3. We have lots of jeans – blue ______ and black ______.
4. Which coat would you like to try on? The long ______ or the short ______?
5. I've brought you two umbrellas – a big ______ and a small ______.
6. Which bag is yours – the black ______ or the brown ______?
7. I like the short coats. The long ______ are too expensive.

41/10b)

9 Work with a partner. Look at the picture and make questions and answers with one or ones.

Example:

A: Where are the red T-shirts?
B: They're next to the green ones.

A: I like this green T-shirt.
B: Yes, I like the green one too.

41/11

1 (SPEAKING) Talk about job ads.

Look at the two job ads. Which job would you prefer? Why / why not? Talk to a partner.

Burger Restaurant
Help wanted!

Working hours:
6 p.m.–10 p.m. (Fridays and Saturdays)
Sell food and clean tables.
Wages: $12 an hour
Work with a friendly and busy team.

Jim's Garden Center
Help wanted!

Working hours:
10 a.m.–3 p.m. (Saturdays and Sundays)
Take care of the plants and help customers.
Wages: $10 an hour
Work inside and outside.

- I'd like to work at ... because ...
- I like working with people.
- I want / don't want to work on weekends.
- I think the wages are ...
- I like / don't like ...
- I'm a friendly / hard-working / ... person.
- I am always polite.
- I like / don't like plants.
- I am good with plants.
- ...

Example:
Partner A: I would like to work at Burger Restaurant because I really like working in a team.
Partner B: I would like to work at Jim's Garden Center because I like working with plants.
Partner A: I am not very good with plants, but I am good with customers.
Partner B: I really like working outside.
Partner A: I don't want to work outside.
...

43/5

1 (READING) Read the comic strip.

2 (READING) Answer the questions.

43/5

1. What are the names of the two high schools?

____

2. Who is Henry? ______________________________
3. What are the two friends doing at Kennedy High School at night?

____

4. Why are the Kennedy High School players so angry?

____

5. Who wins the last game? ______________________________
6. Is Henry dead? ______________________________

3 Think of a good title for the comic strip.

43/5

These words can help you:

chicken | football | mascot | ...

INTERNET

Der Mofaführerschein

Der Mofaführerschein ermöglicht Jugendlichen mehr Freiheit und Unabhängigkeit. Für den Mofaführerschein muss man mindestens 15 Jahre alt sein. Das Mofa darf höchstens 50 ccm Hubraum haben (bei einem Verbrennungsmotor) und nicht schneller als 25 km/h fahren.
Den Mofaführerschein kann man entweder in der Fahrschule oder seltener auch an der Schule machen. Die Kosten setzen sich zusammen aus:

→ 6 Theoriestunden
→ 1 Praxisfahrstunde
→ Theoretische Prüfung

Da die Ausbildung immer gleich abläuft, verlangen die Fahrschulen eine Pauschale. Die Kosten für einen bei der Fahrschule gemachten Mofaführerschein bewegen sich zwischen 70 und 150 €.
Die andere Option ist, den Führerschein in der Schule zu machen. Dies wird jedoch nur von wenigen Schulen angeboten, denn die Ausbildung muss ein extra dafür ausgebildeter Lehrer leiten. Der Mofaführerschein an der Schule ist aber meistens viel günstiger als bei einer Fahrschule, hier muss man mit ca. 30 – 50 € rechnen.

44/2

1 (MEDIATION) Answer the questions in English.

1. How old must you be to get this driver's license? ______
2. Do you have to go to a driving school to get the license? ______
______
3. Is there a practical test or a written test? ______
4. How much does a driver's license cost at a driving school? ______
______

44/2

2 (MEDIATION) At the driving school

Du nimmst einen amerikanischen Austauschschüler mit in die Fahrschule, in der du gerade deinen Mofaführerschein machst. Vermittle zwischen ihm und dem Fahrlehrer.

Student: I'd like to get a driver's license for a moped too. Do I have to be a German citizen?

You: ______
______

Instructor: Nein. Er kann er die schriftliche Prüfung auch auf Englisch machen.

You: ______

Instructor: Hier ist eine Broschüre darüber.

You: ______

Ziel 1: Ich kann Informationen über den Mittleren Westen verstehen

The Midwest is a big area of the USA. Native Americans lived there until more and more European settlers moved West in the 1840s. They were looking for land and gold and often made the Native Americans move away or even killed them. Many Native Americans had to sell their land and move to reservations. Today most of the land in the Midwest is farmland but there are also some big cities. The largest city in the Midwest is Chicago. It is in the state of Illinois and is the third largest city in the USA.
Chicago is often called 'The Windy City'. In 1884 the world's first skyscraper was built here. The Midwest has terrible tornadoes. They are so dangerous that people hide in safe places until the tornado is gone. Because of the great distances in the Midwest, most teenagers want to have their own car. They usually get their driver's license at the age of 16 and often have jobs to save money for a car.

Answer the questions.

1. Why did the European settlers move West? ____________________
2. What did many Native Americans have to do? ____________________
3. What is the largest city in the Midwest? ____________________
4. What is dangerous in the Midwest? ____________________
5. Why do teenagers in the Midwest want to have a car? ____________________

5P
→ p. 34/1

Ziel 2: Ich kann das Schulleben in den USA und in Deutschland vergleichen.

Read the text. Then finish the table with facts about the two schools.

At Anne-Frank-Gesamtschule there are eight classes a day. At Robinson High School there are six classes a day. The school day at the German school starts with the first class. At Robinson High School the school day starts with the Pledge of Allegiance. The school days in Germany and the USA end at 4 p.m. Robinson High School has a dress code and there are a lot of strict rules.

Anne-Frank-Gesamtschule	Robinson High School
eight classes a day	

6P
→ p. 34/2

Ziel 3: Ich kann über Schülerjobs sprechen.

Read the job ad and complete the dialogue.

Help wanted at Tony's Clothes Store

Job for students
weekends 10 a.m.–4 p.m.
$12 an hour
help customers and tidy up the clothes

Billy: Where do you work?

Michael: I work ______________________________.

Billy: Do you work there every day?

Michael: No, ______________________________

Billy: What do you have to do there?

Michael: ______________________________.

Billy: Cool. How much ______________________________?

Michael: ______________________________. I'm saving most of it because I want to buy a car.

5P → p. 35/3

Ziel 4: Ich kann einen Comic über das Highschool-Leben verstehen.

Read the comic strip on pages 28–29 again. What happened first? What happened next? Put the sentences in the right order.

- ☐ The other team can't find their mascot.
- ☐ Robinson High School won a game.
- ☐ The Robinson High player says that they need a new mascot.
- ☐ Henry escaped.
- ☐ A football player kissed Henry.
- ☐ The players stole Henry.
- ☐ Robinson High School lost another game.
- ☐ A cheerleader ate a chicken.
- ☐ Two players planned to steal Henry.

9P → p. 35/4

Ziel 5: Ich kann Informationen über den Führerschein weitergeben.

Six steps to your driver's license

Are you nervous about getting your driver's license?
Here are some tips.

1. Are you sure you are old enough?

In the US every state has its own rules about when you can start learning. For example, in South Dakota you can start getting your license when you are 14, but in New Jersey you have to be 17.

2. Join a Driver's Ed course.

You will learn the rules of the road and how to drive safely.
You can do this at a school or online.

3. Get in the car and start practising!

You must have lessons with a teacher, and the number of hours is not the same in every state.

4. Get extra practice with your family.

The more hours you practise, the better you will be.

5. Take the written test.

Test that you know the rules, and test your eyes.

6. Take your driving test.

This is a little scary, but if you practise enough before the test you will be fine!

Lies den Text und beantworte die Fragen auf Deutsch.

1. Wie alt muss man sein, um den Führerschein in den USA zu machen?

____

____

2. Was ist ein „Driver's Ed" course?

____

3. Muss man in eine Fahrschule gehen?

____

4. Wie kann man fahren üben?

____

____

5. Welche Prüfungen muss man machen?

____

5P

→ p. 35/5

Lösungen online
p664qs

○ Ziel 1: Ich kann Informationen über den Mittleren Westen verstehen.

The American Midwest is a big area of flat farmland and small towns. The summers there are very hot and the winters are very cold. There are also dangerous tornadoes there.

European settlers moved to the Midwest in the 19th century. They wanted land and gold. The Native Americans who lived in the Midwest had to sell their land and move to reservations.

High school students in the USA often have jobs. They work in restaurants, stores or cafés. Many students want to earn money because they want to buy a car.

Every year the new school year starts with Homecoming. Old students return to their high schools. There is a football game and a dance.

Read the text and complete the sentences.

1. The American Midwest is a big area ______________________.
2. They have dangerous ______________________.
3. The European settlers wanted ______________________.
4. The Native Americans had to sell their land and ______________________.
5. Many students have jobs because they want to ______________________.
6. At Homecoming there is a dance and ______________________.

○ Ziel 2: Ich kann das Schulleben in den USA und in Deutschland vergleichen.

Complete the sentences.

principal	Pledge of Allegiance	dress code
In German schools	than in German schools	school bus

American schools are often bigger than German ones. There are usually more clubs in American schools ______________. Every morning, US students must say the ______________ ______________ and the ______________ talks to the students. Most US students go to school by ______________. ______________ students can usually wear what they like but students at American high schools must follow a ______________.

Ziel 3: Ich kann über Schülerjobs sprechen.

Read the job ad and complete the dialogue. Then practise the dialogue.

Your friend: Where is the job?

You: It's at ______________________.

Your friend: What are the working hours?

You: The working hours are ______________________.

Your friend: What days do you have to work?

You: From ______________________.

Your friend: What do you have to do there?

You: I have to ______________________.

Your friend: How much do you make?

You: The wages are ______________________.

Tina's Café
Help wanted!

Working hours:
5 p.m.–8 p.m. (from Monday to Friday)
Sell food and clean tables
Wages: $10 an hour

Ziel 4: Ich kann einen Comic über das Highschool-Leben verstehen.

Read the text on pages 42–43 in your book again. Tick the right box.

	right	wrong
1. Dylan liked Abby but he was too shy to ask her out.	☐	☐
2. Abby's boyfriend was Dylan's best friend.	☐	☐
3. Dylan helped Abby with her English homework.	☐	☐
4. Abby helped Dylan when her boyfriend pushed him.	☐	☐
5. Dylan asked Abby to go to the dance with him.	☐	☐
6. Dylan kissed Abby in front of her house.	☐	☐

Ziel 5: Ich kann Informationen über den Führerschein weitergeben.

Lies dir den Flyer durch und beantworte die Fragen auf Deutsch.

Driver's License

Are you over 15? Are you tired of asking Mom and Dad to give you a ride?

Then learn to drive!

Join our Driver's Ed courses and practise with one of our cars.
All our cars are less than three years old, and all our teachers are friendly.
You can take the written tests right here.

1. Wie alt muss man für die Fahrschule sein? ______
2. Wie kann man fahren üben?
____
____
3. Was gibt es für Autos?
____
____
4. Wo kann den schrifltichen Test machen?
____

LIFE IN TORNADO ALLEY

Tornadoes happen all over the world, and here in the Midwest we know a lot about them. 'Tornado Alley' is the name of an area in the Midwest that goes from West Texas to North Dakota. There can be as many as 200 tornadoes a year here.

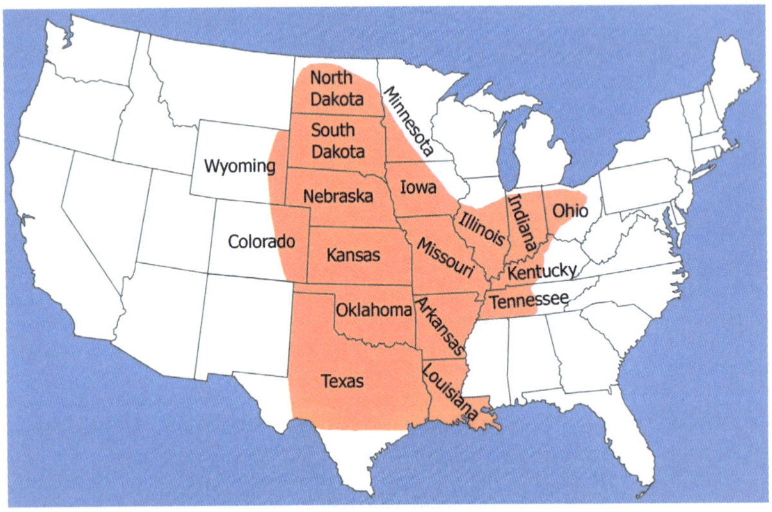

What is a tornado?

A tornado is one of the world's most dangerous weather events. Tornadoes, or twisters, are columns of air which rotate very fast. The winds inside can be almost 500 km/h. This wind can suck up things, animals and even people. Sometimes they destroy streets and houses. Tornadoes are very dangerous and unpredictable. We still don't understand how a tornado happens. Sometimes they are even invisible. Some tornadoes last only 15 minutes, others a few hours.

What should I do if I am near a tornado?

If there is a tornado near you, you will hear about it on the radio or TV. Make sure you bring things inside which a tornado can suck up, like garden chairs or tables. Then find the safest place in your house. This is usually a basement or a room in your house without windows. Some houses in the Midwest even have special tornado shelters. If you're not at home, find shelter in a school or shopping center. Stay there until the tornado has gone.

51/4

1 Read the website. Then match the words.

1. column	aufsaugen
2. to rotate	unsichtbar
3. to suck up	Keller
4. to destroy	Säule
5. unpredictable	rotieren
6. invisible	Schutzraum
7. basement	zerstören
8. shelter	nicht vorhersagbar

51/4

2 Underline the important information in the text. Then use the information to fill in the prompt cards.

What is a tornado?

When and where?

What should you do?

51/4

3 Prepare and give your presentation.

a) Prepare your poster, transparency or computer presentation. Find pictures on the internet which you can use for your presentation.
b) Practise with family or friends.
c) Give your presentation. The words in the boxes will help you.

My presentation is about … | First, I'd like to talk about … | My next topic is … | Now I am going to talk about … | One interesting fact is that … | Finally …

Snow days in the Midwest – a thing of the past?

Every winter the Midwest gets a lot of snow. States like Iowa and Minnesota can get up to one meter of snowfall per year. Sometimes the snow stays for weeks so it is difficult to drive on the roads. When this happens, high schools sometimes have to close for 'snow days'.

This is usually great news for students, but it can also be a problem. Students in the Midwest have to go to school 180 days a year, so it can mean that vacations are shorter because of the snow days.

However, the internet is changing that. Some high schools give laptops to the students and they are allowed to do schoolwork at home. So far, the reaction of students has been very positive. They think it's OK to stay at home to learn because then their vacations won't be shorter. Some students and parents prefer a real teacher, but there are many others who like working at home. A laptop will never give them detention!

A READING

1 Read the text. Which sentence is correct?

A When there is a lot of snow in the Midwest, some high schools have a special winter vacation. ☐

B When there is bad weather in the Midwest, students at some high schools are allowed to work at home. ☐

C When there is a lot of snow in the Midwest, students at some high schools are allowed to work at home. ☐

2 Read the text again and answer the questions.

1. What do high schools do if there is too much snow on the roads?

______

2. Why can snow days be a problem?

______

3. How can these students learn at home?

______

4. Does every student like learning at home? Why / why not?

______

______

B LISTENING

6 **3 Listen to Kate talking about her job. Which picture is correct?**

6 **4 (LISTENING) Listen again and tick the right box.**

1. Kate works at a …

   a) history museum. ☐ b) science museum. ☐

2. She has to put on a …

   a) uniform. ☐ b) costume. ☐

3. She explains the job of a …

   a) farmer. ☐ b) baker. ☐

4. Kate likes her work because she …

   a) loves acting. ☐ b) can work outside. ☐

5. She doesn't like her costume because it …

   a) is too small. ☐ b) smells bad. ☐

C WRITING

5 Write a text about yourself for a job ad.

You see an ad for a student job at a museum. You think it is interesting. The ad asks you to write an e-mail with a short text about yourself. Write a text with information about yourself: who you are, what adjectives describe you, what you like to do, what you don't like to do. Write about 60 words in your exercise book.

These words can help you:

- I am hard-working / responsible …
- I like working with people.
- I don't like …
- I like working indoors / outdoors.
- I am interested in history and …
- …

Start like this:
Subject: Student job at the museum
Dear Sir of Madam,
I read your ad and am interested in the job at the museum. My name is …

Unit 3
In the Northeast

1 Look at the pictures.

52/2

a) Write a title for each picture.

1 

Beautiful

2 

3 

4 

b) Choose one of the pictures and write about it in your exercise book.

c) Read your text to a partner. Can he / she guess which picture it is?

2 Complete the sentences.

52/2

for important celebrations	old Christian community	pardons a turkey
amazing Niagara Falls	the beaches	creepy movies

1. In the Northeast you can enjoy ______.
2. You can also visit the ______.
3. Americans like to meet with family ______.
4. On Thanksgiving the President ______.
5. The Amish are an ______.
6. A lot of mystery stories and ______ are set in Maine.

7 55/4

1 (LISTENING) Listen to Robert and Jacob.

a) What do they talk about? Tick the right boxes.

b) Listen again. Tick the right box.

	right	wrong
1. Robert is a baseball fan.	☐	☐
2. Robert's son is staying in Hawaii for Thanksgiving.	☐	☐
3. Grandfather is sleeping in Jacob's room.	☐	☐
4. Jacob can't play computer games in his room.	☐	☐
5. Jacob is looking forward to the apple pie.	☐	☐
6. Robert usually cooks at Thanksgiving.	☐	☐
7. Jacob wants to have dinner on the sofa.	☐	☐

55/5

2 What can you say in these situations?

Nice to meet you too. | I'm fine, thanks. ✓ | She's fine, thanks. | That's a good idea. | Not much. | Thank you.

1. Hi. How are you doing? I'm fine, thanks.
2. So what have you been up to? ______
3. Nice to meet you. ______
4. I've brought you some chocolates. ______
5. How about watching TV? ______
6. How is your mom? ______

3 Find the signal words for the simple present and the simple past.

56/7

a) Read the dialogue and underline the signal words.

Julia: Do you usually spend Thanksgiving with your mom?

Evan: I often spend Thanksgiving with her. But last year I spent Thanksgiving with my dad.

Julia: Do you always have turkey at Thanksgiving?

Evan: No, I often eat vegetables because my mom is a vegetarian.

Julia: Oh, Jacob is a vegetarian too. I sometimes make a Thanksgiving dinner without meat. Two years ago we had two salads. But the rest of the family often wants a turkey during the holidays. Yesterday I made a vegetable pie for our Thanksgiving dinner.

b) Write the signal words in the table.

simple present	simple past
usually	

4 Make questions in the right tense.

56/7

a) Write the questions.

b) Write your own answers to the questions.

1. you • go on holiday • last year?
   Did you go on holiday last year? ___ Yes, I did.
2. your dad • often • cook dinner?
   ___ ___
3. you • go out • yesterday?
   ___ ___
4. your mom • watch the news • last night?
   ___ ___
5. you • always • get presents at Christmas?
   ___ ___
6. you • sometimes • eat chocolate for dinner?
   ___ ___

Do you like chocolate?
– Yes, I do. / No, I don't.

Does she like chocolate?
– Yes, she does. / No, she doesn't.

Did you eat some chocolate yesterday?
– Yes, I did. / No, I didn't.

56/8a)

5 Use the words to make questions in the present and past.

Where	do you	usually	go	after school	last year
Who	did you	often	eat	on your birthday	yesterday
What		always	drink	at Christmas	last week
		never	do	at Thanksgiving	
			meet	on the weekend	
			call		
			visit		

1. Where do you usually go after school? / Where did you go after school yesterday?
2.
3.
4.
5.
6.
7.

57/9a)

6 Write questions for the underlined answers.

1. Thanksgiving was really great last year.
2. We spent the holidays at my grandma's house.
3. All the family was there.
4. We always have turkey for dinner.
5. We celebrated there because my grandma is afraid of flying.
6. I think I'll visit my grandma at Christmas again.
7. I always enjoy the holidays.
8. I think I'll invite my boyfriend.

1. What was really great last year?
2. Where did
3. Who
4. What
5. Why
6. When
7. What
8. Who

1 Give an opinion.

59/5a)

a) Work with a partner. One partner reads a sentence.
The other partner uses a phrase from the list to agree or disagree

That's true. | I don't think so. | Exactly. | Absolutely not. | No way. | That's for sure.

1. It is more fun hanging out with friends than spending time with your family.
2. Gossip magazines can be really awful.
3. People spend too much time on their phones.
4. There are more important things to do than buy a new phone every year.
5. It must be difficult to live like the Amish.
6. Computers make most things easier.
7. Fashion is a really interesting topic.

59/5b)

b) Choose two of the sentences above and write your opinion about them.

I'm convinced that | I guess | It's clear to me that | I doubt that

I'm convinced that gossip magazines are awful because

2 Which device is it?

59/6

Look at the picture and choose one device. Describe it to your partner but don't say the name.
Let your partner guess what it is. Take turns. The words in the boxes can help you.

You use it to … | It is small/big. | It is a thing that … | It is black and red.

8 59/6

3 (LISTENING) Listen to Jennifer talking to her mom.

a) Answer the question.
What is their argument about?

____

b) Listen again and fill in the table.

Write two things Jennifer doesn't like about camping.	
Write two things her mom wants to do during their holiday.	
Write one reason why her mom wants to go camping.	

60/7

4 Complete the sentences.

1. If I *lived* (live) in the USA, I would speak English perfectly.
2. If I __________ (go) to the USA, I would try some American food.
3. If I __________ (move) to the USA, I would miss my friends.
4. If I __________ (have) a garden, I would grow my own food.
5. If you __________ (visit) the USA, you would find out about life there.
6. If you __________ (be) Amish, you wouldn't have any technology.
7. If Jennifer __________ (not have) her phone, she would be really unhappy.
8. If Ruth __________ (leave) the community, she would miss her family.

Du verwendest im if-Satz simple past: lived, went, had

60/7

5 Complete the sentences.

1. If I were Amish, I __________ (not use) make-up.
2. If Jennifer went camping, she __________ (miss) her phone.
3. If Ruth lived in the outside world, she __________ (not cover) her hair.
4. If you didn't have a phone, you __________ (write) more postcards.
5. If your friend asked you for help, you __________ (help) her.
6. If you used a hair straightener, you hair __________ (look) better.
7. If we didn't stop my mom, she __________ (go) camping every year.

Im Hauptsatz steht would / wouldn't + Grundform des Verbs: would use, wouldn't use

60/8a)

6 Match the pictures with the sentences. Then complete the sentences.

she had her own horse.

she didn't grow vegetables.

she would miss her family.

she wouldn't need a candle.

she left the community.

she would watch TV with her.

1. Ruth wouldn't have a lot of food if she didn't
2. She would feel very lonely if
3. If she had electricity,
4. If she lived in Jennifer's house,
5. If she lived in the outside world,
6. She would get around quicker if

61/9a)

7 (YOUR TURN) Complete the sentences with your own ideas.

1. I would be very angry if
2. I would be surprised if
3. I would be very happy if
4. I would speak English more if
5. I would be scared if

61/9b)

8 (YOUR TURN) What would you do if ...?

a) Write four questions for your partner.

be 18 years old | meet your favorite star | go back in time | ...

1. What would you do if you were 18 years old?
2.
3.
4.

b) Write your partner's answers in your exercise book.

61/10

1 Act small talk conversations.

a) Work in a group of four. Each of you chooses one of the cards. Read the information on your card.

Brianna

You are 15 years old.
You are very friendly.
You have a cat called Lizzy.
Your hobbies are reading and swimming.
You are meeting Lea for the first time.
Ask Lea how she is doing.
Ask Lea where she comes from.
Talk about your hobbies and pet.

Lea

You are 16 years old.
You are an exchange student from Berlin.
You are staying with Brianna's neighbors.
Your hobbies are dancing and rock climbing.
In Germany you have a dog called Tommy.
You are meeting the others for the first time.
Talk about your hobbies and pet.

Nick

You are 17 years old.
You are Brianna's neighbor.
You are bored because your brother is using your computer.
Your hobby is playing computer games.
Say how bored you are and why.
Say that you often go to the movies.
Agree to play basketball with Tom.

Tom

You are 16 years old.
You are Nick's friend.
You have just arrived at Nick's house.
Say that you want to play basketball with Nick.
Say that you want to go to the movies on Saturday.
Invite Lea to go to the movies with you.

b) You are meeting the other three at Nick's house. Act small talk conversations.

Hi. How are you?	I'm fine, thanks. How are you?	Where are you from?
What are your hobbies?	I like / I don't like …	I have …
What do you do on …?	Would you like to …?	I often go …

65/6

1 (READING) Read the letters of two young Amish people.

Ruth and Sarah both come from a small Amish community in Pennsylvania. You read about Ruth on page 58 of your book. Ruth is very happy in her Amish community, but Sarah has decided that she wants to spend more time in the outside world. Sarah now lives with a family in the city Philadelphia. The two friends write letters to each other.

Ruth

Sarah

July 31st

Dear Ruth,
How are you? I still can't believe you chose to stay in the community. Philadelphia is amazing but it's also loud and dirty and has lots of people. The kids I look after in my guest family are really cool, and I have a lot of free time. At first I watched TV and surfed the internet all the time, and I ate so much ice cream that I was sick. But that got boring so now I have a new job in a clothes store on Saturdays. At first it was strange to see all these people who bought clothes and make-up all the time. On Saturday evenings I often go out with my co-workers, but I usually spend Sundays with my guest family. We're going to go to New York next week and I'm super excited! I'll tell you all about it in my next letter.
Love, Sarah

August 10th

Dear Sarah,
Thank you for your letter. I hope you enjoyed New York. I also have some great news – Samuel and I are going to get married! I'm so happy! We haven't chosen a date yet and Father wants me to wait till I'm 18 anyway, so I guess the wedding will be next summer. I really hope you will be back by then.
Love, Ruth

August 19th

Dear Ruth,
Congratulations! I still can't believe you're getting married. You're my friend and of course I'm happy for you … I'm having so much fun here. Last Saturday I met a really nice boy and at the end of the evening he kissed me in his car. I feel that I can be the person I want to be for the first time in my life.
Love, Sarah

August 28th

Dear Sarah,
I really miss you! Mother and I are very busy at the moment. We are cooking and putting food away for the winter. I can't wait for next Sunday because Samuel is coming over from his community. Please write soon and tell me more about your life in the city. It all sounds very exciting!
Love, Ruth

G2 Mit G sind die Grammatikkapitel gekennzeichnet und der Reihe nach durchnummeriert.

G6 Language tip: Die Seiten kennzeichnen zusätzliche Grammatikkapitel. Du kannst dir die neuen Formen dort wie neue Vokabeln merken oder – wenn du es genau wissen willst – ein paar Regeln dazu lernen.

G1 Die einfache Vergangenheit

Das Grammatikkapitel zur einfachen Vergangenheit findest du im Blue Line 1 Workbook.

G2 Die Vorvergangenheit

The past perfect

After I had built my new house, I felt much better.

Um über Ereignisse zu sprechen, die noch **vor** einem vergangenen Ereignis stattfanden, verwendest du die Vorvergangenheit, das **past perfect: had / hadn't + 3. Form** des Verbs (past participle).

Signalwörter	
after	nachdem
before	bevor

Bei den meisten Verben hängst du für die 3. Form ein **-ed** an das Verb: visit → visited
Achte auf unregelmäßige Verben, z. B. go → **gone**; see → **seen**; be → **been** etc.

Eine Liste der unregelmäßigen Verben findest du ab Seite 217.

Was in der Vergangenheit weiter zurückliegt, wird mit dem **past perfect** ausgedrückt!

She wasn't at home. She **had gone** to Tim's (house).	Sie war nicht zu Hause. Sie war zu Tim gegangen.
After I **had been** in NYC for two months, I moved to Chicago.	Nachdem ich zwei Monate in NYC gewesen war, zog ich nach Chicago um.
I **hadn't seen** skyscrapers before I went to New York.	Ich hatte noch keine Wolkenkratzer gesehen, bevor ich nach New York ging.

Und so kannst du im **past perfect** Fragen stellen:

Had you ever **been** to the USA before you left Cuba?	Yes, I **had**.	No, I **hadn't**.
Which countries **had** you **visited** before you went to the USA?	I **hadn't visited** any other countries at all.	

G3 Modale Hilfsverben und ihre Ersatzformen

Modal auxiliaries and their substitutes

Can und **must** kannst du nur im **simple present** verwenden. Für alle anderen Zeiten, z. B. für das **simple past**, benötigst du **Ersatzformen.**

Mit **can** und der Ersatzform **be able to** sagst du, was du tun **kannst** (Fähigkeit).

Simple present	Simple past
Kim **can** speak English.	Kim **was able to** understand it.
Kim **kann** Englisch sprechen.	Kim **konnte** es verstehen.
Can your friend speak English?	**Was** she **able to speak** English?
Kann dein Freund Englisch sprechen?	**Konnte** sie Englisch sprechen?

Mit **can** und der Ersatzform **be allowed to** sagst du, was du tun **darfst** (Erlaubnis).

She **can't** use her phone.	She **wasn't allowed to** use it.
Sie **darf** ihr Handy **nicht** benutzen.	Sie **durfte** ihr Handy **nicht** benutzen.
Can you wear jeans?	**Were** you **allowed to** wear jeans?
Darfst du Jeans tragen?	**Durftest** du Jeans tragen?

Mit **must** und der Ersatzform **have to** sagst du, was du tun **musst** (Verpflichtung).

Sarah **must** take English and History.	Sarah **had to** take Biology too.
Sarah **muss** Englisch und Geschichte nehmen.	Sarah **musste** auch Biologie nehmen.
We **don't have to** worry.	We **didn't have to** worry.
Wir **müssen** uns keine Sorgen machen.	Wir **mussten** uns **keine Sorgen** machen.
Must you help your parents?	**Did** you **have to** help in the house?
Musst du deinen Eltern helfen?	**Musstest** du im Haus helfen?

Bei **must** musst du die Ersatzform schon in **verneinten Sätzen** im **simple present** benutzen!

G4 Bedingungssätze Typ I

Das Grammatikkapitel zu den Bedingungssätzen Typ I findest du im Blue Line 3 Workbook.

G5 Stützwort one / ones

One / ones

Um eine unnötige Wiederholung von Nomen zu vermeiden, kannst du sie durch **one** (Einzahl) und **ones** (Mehrzahl) ersetzen. **One / ones** werden nicht übersetzt. Sie stehen oft nach einem Adjektiv. Auch nach der Steigerungsform eines Adjektivs kommt **one** oder **ones** häufig vor.

Who are those boys over there?	Wer sind diese Jungs dort drüben?
The tall ~~boy~~ **one** is Jim and the short ~~boy~~ **one** is Tim.	Der große ~~Junge~~ ist Jim und der kleine ~~Junge~~ ist Tim.
Which towels did you buy?	Welche Handtücher hast du gekauft?
– The cheaper **ones.**	– Die billigeren.
Which books do you prefer?	Welche Bücher bevorzugst du?
– Exciting **ones.**	– Spannende.

G6 Language tip: Bestätigungsfragen

Question tags

You didn't eat the turkey, did you?

Um ein Gespräch nicht abreißen zu lassen, kannst du eine Bestätigungsfrage (question tag) benutzen. Im Deutschen sagt man dafür Ausdrücke wie **nicht wahr?**, **nicht?**, **oder?**
Für negative **question tags** benutzt du immer Kurzformen.
Alle **question tags** werden mit einem Komma vom Aussagesatz abgetrennt.

Ist der Aussagesatz positiv +, so wird die Bestätigungsfrage negativ –.

Aussagesatz +	Question tag –
It's cold,	**isn't** it?
You **are** fifteen,	**aren't** you?
She **can** play the guitar,	**can't** she?
Robert **was** in Boston,	**wasn't** he?
You **were** in New York,	**weren't** you?

Ist der Aussagesatz negativ –, so wird die Bestätigungsfrage positiv +.

Aussagesatz –	Question tag +
Your shirt **isn't** new,	**is** it?
You **weren't** in the USA last year,	**were** you?

Bei Vollverben musst du **do**, **does**, **did** oder **don't**, **doesn't**, **didn't** benutzen:

You **like** chocolates,	**don't** you?
Julia **wants** to go to Miami,	**doesn't** she?
You **met Brenda**,	**didn't** you?
You **don't like** turkey,	**do** you?
Nick **doesn't drink** coke,	**does** he?
Robert **didn't see** the Niagara Falls,	**did** he?

G7 Fragen

Questions / questions with who

So bildest du unterschiedliche Fragen mit Vollverben, z. B. like, go etc.:

Fragen, auf die man mit yes oder no antwortet (Ja/Nein-Fragen)
– Fragen im **simple present** beginnst du mit **do** oder **does** (he, she, it).

Do you **like** turkey?	Magst du Truthahn?
Does Jacob **like** chocolate?	Mag Jacob Schokolade?

– Fragen im **simple past** beginnst du mit **did** für alle Personen.

Did you **travel** by car last year?	Bist du letztes Jahr mit dem Auto verreist?
Did it **rain** last December?	Hat es im letzten Dezember geregnet?

– Fragen im **will-future** beginnst du mit **will** für alle Personen.

Will you **call** us again tomorrow?	Wirst du uns morgen nochmal anrufen?

Fragen mit Fragewörtern

What do you **like**?	Was magst du gerne?
Where did you **spend** your summer?	Wo hast du deinen Sommer verbracht?
When will you **go** to Boston?	Wann wirst du nach Boston fahren?

Fragen mit who
– Das Fragewort **who?** kann **verschiedene Bedeutungen** haben:
– Heißt es **Wer?** wird **keine Form von do** verwendet.
– Heißt es **Wen?** oder **Wem?** muss **eine Form von do** verwendet werden.

Who lives in Boston?	**Wer** lebt in Boston?
Who do you **like**?	**Wen** magst du?
Who did you **help** last week?	**Wem** hast du letzte Woche geholfen?

Präpositonen bleiben in Fragen meistens beim Verb stehen. Im Deutschen dagegen steht die Präposition meistens beim Fragewort. Vergleiche:

Who did you **talk to?**	**Mit wem** hast du dich unterhalten?
Where do you **come from?**	**Woher** kommst du?

G8 Bedingungssätze Typ II

Das Grammatikkapitel zu den Bedingungssätzen Typ II findest du im Blue Line 3 Workbook.

G9 Gegenüberstellung: Simple present - present progressive

Das Grammatikkapitel zu den Gegenwartszeiten findest du im Blue Line 3 Workbook.

G10 Adjektive und Adverbien

Das Grammatikkapitel zu Adjektiven und Adverbien findest du in den Blue Line 2 + 3 Workbooks.

G11 Das Perfekt

The present perfect

Wenn eine Handlung in der Vergangenheit beginnt und in der Gegenwart zu einem Ergebnis führt, verwendest du das **present perfect**:
have/has + 3. Form des Verbs (past participle).
Bei den meisten Verben hängst du ein **-ed** an das Verb: help → help**ed**

Eine Liste der unregelmäßigen Verben findest du ab Seite 217.

Signalwörter	
already	schon
just	gerade
not … yet	noch … nicht
never	noch nie
ever (in Fragen)	jemals (in Fragen)
since	seit (Zeitpunkt)
for	seit (Zeitspanne)

Einige Verben haben unregelmäßige 3. Formen: z. B. be → **been**; write → **written**

I **have** just **posted** a photo.	Ich habe gerade ein Foto verschickt.
She **has** already **written** ten text messages.	Sie hat schon zehn SMS geschrieben.

Um Sätze zu verneinen, benutzt du **haven't** oder **hasn't** (bei he, she, it):

I **haven't been** to California yet.	Ich bin noch nicht in Kalifornien gewesen.
She **hasn't seen** Los Angeles yet.	Sie hat Los Angeles noch nicht gesehen.

Fragen und Kurzantworten bildest du so:

Have you ever **been** to San Francisco?	Yes, I **have**.	No, I **haven't**.
Has your sister ever **met** a famous star?	Yes, she **has**.	No, she **hasn't**.

Present perfect mit **for** und **since**
since (**seit**) verwendest du vor einem **Zeitpunkt**, z. B. **since** 5 o'clock, **since** July, **since** 2013.
for (**seit**) verwendest du vor einer **Zeitspanne**, z. B. **for** five hours, **for** three years, **for** a long time.

I haven't seen Lara **since** Monday.	Ich habe Lara **seit** Montag nicht gesehen.
I haven't seen Lara **for** a week.	Ich habe Lara **seit** einer Woche nicht gesehen.

Im Deutschen verwendet man oft die **Gegenwart**, wenn man sagen will, seit wann oder wie lange etwas schon andauert. Vergleiche:

I **have lived** in Los Angeles for two years.	Ich **lebe seit** zwei Jahren in Los Angeles.
She **has had** a smartphone since last year.	Sie **hat seit** letztem Jahr ein Smartphone.

G12 Das Passiv

Passive voice (simple present and simple past)

English is important.
It is spoken all over the world.

Mit dem Passiv kannst du über eine Handlung Auskunft geben, ohne zu sagen, wer die Handlung ausführt. Im Vordergrund steht die Handlung.

So bildest du das **Passiv** im **simple present: am / are / is + 3. Form des Verbs** (past participle)

English **is spoken** in a lot of countries.	Englisch **wird** in vielen Ländern **gesprochen**.
Racism **isn't accepted**.	Rassismus **wird nicht akzeptiert**.
Spices and flour **are mixed**.	Gewürze und Mehl **werden gemischt**.

So bildest du das Passiv im **simple past: was / were + 3. Form des Verbs** (past participle)

Raleigh **was founded** in the 18th century.	Raleigh **wurde** im 18. Jahrhundert **gegründet**.
The airport **wasn't finished** until 1929.	Der Flughafen **wurde nicht** vor 1929 **fertiggestellt**.
The streets **were built** in a special way.	Die Straßen **wurden** auf besondere Weise **gebaut**.

Willst du in einem Passivsatz sagen, **wer** die Handlung ausführt, ergänzt du ihn oder sie mit **by**.

The city of Raleigh **was founded by** the French.	Die Stadt Raleigh **wurde von** den Franzosen **gegründet**.
New dishes **were brought** here **by** the slaves.	Neue Gerichte **wurden von** den Sklaven hierher **gebracht**.

G13 Indirekte Rede (ohne Zeitverschiebung)

Reported speech (without backshift)

Oh no! Dad says we have to take a shower now!

Mit der indirekten Rede kannst du über das berichten, was jemand anderes **gerade gesagt hat**. Du beginnst mit **He says that . . . / She says that . . .** usw. Das Wort **that** kann man auch weglassen.

Positive Aussagen und verneinte Sätze in der indirekten Rede bildest du so:

Direkte Rede	Indirekte Rede
Anna says, "**I like** Florida."	Anna says (that) **she likes** Florida.
Anna says, "**We want** to see the alligators."	Anna says (that) **they want** to see the alligators.
Anna says, "**I don't need** a hotel."	Anna says (that) **she doesn't need** a hotel.

Beachte die Änderungen:

I	→ **he/she**	**my**	→ **his/her**
we	→ **they**	**our**	→ **their**
(I) **like**	→ (he/she) **likes**		
(I) **don't . . .**	→ (he/she) **doesn't . . .**		

Fragen in der indirekten Rede werden so wiedergegeben:

Du beginnst z. B. mit	**She asks if . . .**	Sie fragt, **ob . . .**
Bei Fragen mit Fragewörtern beginnst du z. B. mit	**He asks where . . .**	Er fragt, **wo/wohin . . .**

Direkte Rede	Indirekte Rede
Anna asks Ethan, "**Do you like** alligators?"	She asks Ethan **if he likes** alligators.
Nick asks, "**Where do you go** camping?"	He asks **where they go** camping.

Erkenne die Zeitform in der **Frage** der direkten Rede (hier: **simple present**) und bilde in der indirekten Rede einen **Satz** im **simple present** nach der Regel **S**ubjekt – **V**erb – **O**bjekt!

G14 Indirekte Rede (mit Zeitverschiebung)

Reported speech (with backshift)

Look, I've got a new boyfriend.
But he's a bat!
And he told me he was a pilot.

Mit der indirekten Rede kannst du über etwas berichten, was jemand **vor einiger Zeit gesagt hat.** Du beginnst mit **He said that ...** / **She told me that ...** usw. Das Wort **that** kann man auch weglassen. Das Verb des Satzes wird vom **simple present** in das **simple past** zurückgesetzt. Das nennt man **backshift**.
Backshift gilt auch für die Verneinung: aus **don't** / **doesn't** wird **didn't**.

Positive Aussagen und verneinte Sätze in der indirekten Rede bildest du so:

Direkte Rede	Indirekte Rede
Al Lane said, "I **get up** at 6 a.m."	Al Lane told me (that) he **got up** at 6 a.m.
He said, "There **are** 20 alligators."	He said (that) there **were** 20 alligators.
He said, "We **don't get** a lot of visitors."	He said (that) they **didn't get** a lot of visitors.

2 Complete the sentences.

65/6

1. Ruth is Sarah's …
   a) co-worker. ☐
   b) friend. ☐
   c) sister. ☐

2. Ruth has decided to …
   a) stay in the community. ☐
   b) leave the community. ☐
   c) live with her boyfriend. ☐

3. Sarah is staying …
   a) with a guest family. ☐
   b) in another community. ☐
   c) at home. ☐

4. Sarah has …
   a) one job. ☐
   b) two jobs. ☐
   c) three jobs. ☐

5. Ruth is happy because …
   a) she is going to get married. ☐
   b) she has a new boyfriend. ☐
   c) Sarah is coming home. ☐

6. Sarah wants to go
   a) to Philadelphia. ☐
   b) home. ☐
   c) to New York. ☐

3 Complete the table.

65/6

Sort the facts in the boxes about Ruth and Sarah. Which facts are about Ruth? Which facts are about Sarah? Write the facts in the table.

- is going to New York soon
- lives in an Amish community
- is going to get married
- her boyfriend's name is Samuel
- cooks a lot with her mother
- lives in Philadelphia ✓
- has met a nice boy
- wants to stay in the community
- works in a clothes store
- looks after kids
- goes out on Saturday evenings

Sarah	Ruth
lives in Philadelphia	

4 (WRITING) Write about Ruth or Sarah in your exercise book.

65/6

Use the information in exercise 3 to write about 60 words about Ruth or Sarah.

INTERNET

BUS FACILITIES

Wi-Fi is free on all our buses for all passengers. Please don't stream videos.

You can put your bags in the storage room above your seat.

Our comfortable leather seats are adjustable so that you can relax and sleep.

Alcohol is not allowed on the bus.

Every seat has its own power outlet so you can use and charge your devices during the journey.

On our buses there is always enough room for your legs.

We stop for breaks but it's good to know that there is a toilet on each bus if you need it.

66/2

1 Beantworte die Fragen.

1. Wie sind die Busse ausgestattet? Schreibe drei Sachen auf.

____

____

____

2. Was darf man nicht mit in den Bus nehmen? _______________

66/2

2 At the bus station

Du bist am Busbahnhof in Boston. Eine Frau aus Deutschland braucht Hilfe am Fahrkartenschalter. Vermittle zwischen ihr und dem Verkäufer.

Woman: Hallo, ich möchte gerne eine Gruppenfahrkarte nach Philadelphia kaufen.

You: *She would like to* _______________

Man: OK. How many people are in the group?

You: _______________

Woman: Wir sind zu fünft. Drei Erwachsene und zwei Kinder.

You: _______________

Man: Are any of you over 62? If so, you can get a cheaper ticket too.

You: _______________

____

Woman: Nein. Frag ihn bitte, wieviel die Fahrkarten kosten.

You: _______________

Ziel 1: Ich kann Informationen über den Nordosten der USA verstehen.

The Northeast of America covers a big area. From the big cities of Philadelphia and Boston, the lakes in the north and the famous Niagara Falls, the beautiful beaches on the East Coast to its big forests, there is something for everyone. In the summer you can enjoy the coast and in the winter you can visit the mountains in the north to ski. However, maybe the best times to visit are in the spring, when the mountains of Pennsylvania are full of flowers, and in the fall, when the forests are so colorful that all you can see is orange, red and gold.

Answer the questions.

1. What are two big cities in the Northeast? ______
2. What can you find in the north? ______
3. What can you do in the winter? ______
4. When is the best times to visit the Northeast? ______
5. Why should you visit the Northeast in the fall? ______

______

5P

→ p. 54/1

Ziel 2: Ich kann einen Text ausdrucksstark vorlesen.

Put the symbols into the text. Then read the dialogue with a partner.

voice goes up ↗ | voice goes down ↘

worried | surprised | happy | sad

Emily: Hi Ashley, what's up? ↗

Ashley: Hi, how are you? Where's your brother? Didn't he want to come too?

Emily: Oh, well … Yes, he did but he has broken his arm.

Ashley: Really? Is he OK? How did it happen?

Emily: On his skateboard, of course. He should really be more careful. But it's not too bad, so don't worry. What have you been up to?

Ashley: Not much. I got a new cell phone yesterday. Look, it's cool, isn't it?

Emily: Wow! I love it! If I had some money, I would get a new phone too. Mine is so old.

Ashley: Maybe you should ask your parents for one for your birthday next month?

Emily: Good idea! Oh, the movie is starting. Let's go!

6P

→ p. 54/2

Ziel 3: Ich kann meine Meinung sagen und begründen.

Should students have cell phones in school?

a) Read the reasons for and against.

For	Against
can call or text your parents can search the internet can play games between classes can show photos or videos to your friends	you don't concentrate in classes teachers would be angry can play games if classes are boring would get bad grades someone can steal it from your bag

b) Yes or no? Write your opinion. Look on page 61 of your book for help.

The question is "Should students have cell phones in school?" I

8P

→ p. 55/3

Ziel 4: Ich kann eine Geschichte über Freunde verstehen.

Read the text on page 48 again and answer the questions.

1. Who does Sarah live with in Philadelphia?
2. Why does Sarah have a new job?
3. What is Ruth's great news?
4. How does Sarah feel about Ruth and Samuel?
5. Do Ruth and Samuel live in the same community?

5P

→ p. 55/4

Ziel 5: Ich kann Informationen über Reisemöglichkeiten weitergeben.

INTERNET

▶ **Wednesday, November 16, 2016**
Chicago to **New York City**
9:30 pm-6:23 pm (Thu, Nov 18)
19 hr, 53 min
Value

1 Adult	$106.00
1 Reserved Seat	included
Subtotal	**$106.00**

▶ **Sunday, November 20, 2016**
New York City to **Chicago**
3:40 am-9:45 am (Mon, Nov 20)
19 hr, 53 min
Value

1 Adult	$106.00
1 Reserved Seat	included
Subtotal	**$106.00**
Total	**$212.00**

INTERNET

from **Chicago, IL**
to **New York City, NY**
11 h 27 min without traffic
⚠ **This route has tolls.**

Distance: 790 miles
Price of gas: about $120

a) Lies dir die Internetseiten durch und beantworte die Fragen auf Deutsch.

1. Wie lange dauert die Zugfahrt von New York nach Chicago? ______
2. Was ist billiger, eine Hin- und Rückfahrt mit dem Zug oder mit dem Auto? ______
3. Was geht schneller? ______

b) Du schaust dir den Zugfahrplan zusammen mit deiner amerikanischen Gastmutter und deiner Mutter an, die dich während deines Austauschjahrs in den USA besucht. Vermittle zwischen den beiden.

Your mom: Sag ihr, ich denke, wir sollten mit dem Auto fahren.
You: ______
Guest mom: The journey by car is much shorter. But it is better by train because you can sleep on the train.
You: ______
______
Your mom: Ja, das klingt gut. Was bedeutet eigentlich „This route has tolls"?
You: ______
Guest mom: It means you have to pay when you use some of the roads.
You: ______

7P

→ p. 55/5

Lösungen online
9cs9qk

Ziel 1: Ich kann Informationen über den Nordosten der USA verstehen.

In the Northeast of the USA there is a lot to see. You can visit Niagara Falls on the border to Canada or you can enjoy miles of clean beaches on the Atlantic Coast. In the fall you can see amazing colors when the forests are red, gold and orange.

Thanksgiving is a very important holiday in the USA. Most families spend this holiday together and eat a turkey dinner. Some family members travel long distances because they live so far away. Every year the president pardons a turkey at the White House.

Read the texts and complete the sentences.

1. You can visit Niagara Falls on ______
2. In the fall the forests are ______
3. Most families spend Thanksgiving together and ______
4. Some family members travel long distances because ______
5. Every year the president pardons ______

Ziel 2: Ich kann einen Text ausdrucksstark vorlesen.

Put the symbols into the text. Then read the dialogue with a partner.

voice goes up ↗ | voice goes down ↘ | ☺ happy | 😮 surprised | ☹ sad

Emily: Hi Ashley. How are ↗ you?

Ashley: Hi. I'm fine, thanks.

Emily: Oh, is this your new phone?

Ashley: Yes, it is. It's awesome. I can take great photos with it. Look!

Emily: Cool. I also want a new phone, but I haven't got any money.

Ashley: Don't worry! Maybe your parents will buy you one for your birthday.

Ziel 3: Ich kann meine Meinung sagen und begründen.

Should teenagers have a TV in their room? Choose phrases from below and complete the sentences.

- "Should teenagers have a TV in their room?" ✓
- they would be late for school.
- shouldn't have a TV in their room.
- have a TV in their room.
- had a TV in their room,
- to bed late.
- their homework.

The question is "Should teenagers have a TV in their room?" ______ I don't think teenagers should ______ If they ______ they wouldn't do ______ I also think that they would go ______ If they went to bed late, ______

So all in all they ______

Ziel 4: Ich kann eine Geschichte über Freunde verstehen.

Read the text on pages 62–64 in your book again. Choose the right answer.

	right	wrong
1. The friends go on a trip because they want to find a dead body.	☐	☐
2. Chris's dad gave him the gun.	☐	☐
3. Chris's dad won't miss the gun because he is drunk.	☐	☐
4. There were no bullets in the gun.	☐	☐
5. Chris brought the gun because it's scary in the forest at night.	☐	☐
6. It's a long walk to Harlow.	☐	☐

Ziel 5: Ich kann Informationen über Reisemöglichkeiten weitergeben.

Philadelphia, PA 7:00 a.m.	>	**November 4 (Fri)** 7 h 20 m	>	**Boston, MA** 2:20 p.m.	**Price**	Fare total for 1 Adult $41
					Fees	$5
					Total	**$46**

Schau dir den Busfahrplan an und beantworte die Fragen auf Deutsch.

1. Wohin soll die Fahrt gehen? ______
2. Um wie viel Uhr fährt der Bus ab? ______
3. Wie lange ist man unterwegs? ______
4. Wie viel kostet die Busfahrt insgesamt? ______

INTERNET

Halloween in the USA

Part 1: People all over the world celebrate Halloween on October 31st. In the USA Halloween is a very popular holiday.

Part 2: No one really knows how Halloween started, but many people think it started in Scotland, Wales and Ireland. When a lot of people emigrated from Scotland and Ireland to the USA in the 19th century, Halloween also became popular there. Now almost everyone in the USA puts up Halloween decorations, wears costumes, watches scary movies or goes to parties. There are special parades and people play tricks or try to scare each other.

Part 3: Americans of all ages spend weeks planning their Halloween costumes and many also decorate their houses with scary things. One of the most important traditions is 'trick or treat'. This is when children in costumes go to their neighbors' houses and knock on their doors. Then they say 'trick or treat?' and the people give the children some candy. If they don't, the children will play a trick on them! Another important tradition is to make pumpkin lanterns, or 'jack o'lanterns'. These are pumpkins in which you have carved a scary face and put a candle inside. People put them outside their houses as a sign that children are welcome to ask for candy.

Part 4: A lot of children today have food allergies and can't eat candy, so a lot of people give the children small presents instead, for example plastic jewellery or stickers. As a sign that children will get allergy-free candy or something else, people put a blue pumpkin in front of their house.

73/3 **1** Read the website.

73/3 **2** Look at the pictures and guess the German words.

1. to knock: ____________

2. candy: ____________

3. to carve: ____________

4. lantern: ____________

73/3 ↗ **3 Find important information on the website.**

a) Underline the important information.
b) Write notes for each part of the text. Write two or three facts for each part.

Part 1 Halloween in the USA on October 31st

Part 2

Part 3

Part 4

73/3 ↗ **4 Use your notes to write a summary in your exercise book.**

The website is about …	It explains / describes …
Another … is ..	There is also …
First / Second / Third …	Finally …
Talks about …	I think …
Then / After that …	In my opinion …

Wenn du einen Text zusammenfasst, benutzt du normalerweise das simple present. Benutze das simple past nur, wenn du über vergangene Ereignisse schreibst.

Start like this:

The website is about Halloween in the USA. It is

73/3 ↗ **5 Check your summary. Use the list on page 179 in your book for help.**

Unit 4

California dreams

74/2

1 Find the words.

You have found this brochure on the internet but some words are not there. There are just symbols. Can you guess the words? Each symbol is a different letter. For example, the symbol □ is the letter d. The first letter of each word is there. Write the correct words over the symbols.

California Tours

Our great tour starts in sunny Los Angeles.

We are going to visit a movie s ✱ ♦ □ ⌘ ▶ where you can see the very exciting world of the m ▶ ⩔ ⌘ 🌢 i ⊙ □ ♦ ⅄ ✱ ■ ● .

Later you can find your favorite star on the Walk of Fame. They are all there!

In the afternoon you can enjoy the r 🌢 ★ ✦ ✪ 🌢 □ California lifestyle on the beach.

On our second day we are going to visit San Fransisco, where you can take a r ⌘ □ 🌢 on an old c ✦ ♥ ★ 🌢 c ✦ ■ . Then we are going to go to a park with giant r 🌢 □ ⁘ ▶ ▶ □ trees. In the afternoon we will go to Silicon Valley, where a number of high-t 🌢 ✕ ☼ companies have s 🌢 ✱ ✱ ★ 🌢 □ .

74/2

2 Search the internet and find the answers to the questions.

1. How many people live in California? ______
2. What are the three largest cities in California? ______
3. Today California has more immigrants than any other state in the USA. Where do most of them come from? ______

76/2

1 Complete the crossword.

1. a journey with a guide
2. when you book something you make a …
3. the way you live
4. a very small mountain
5. there are lots of … cars in San Francisco
6. someone who designs houses is an …
7. very high
8. to put color on something
9. when you make a reservation you … something

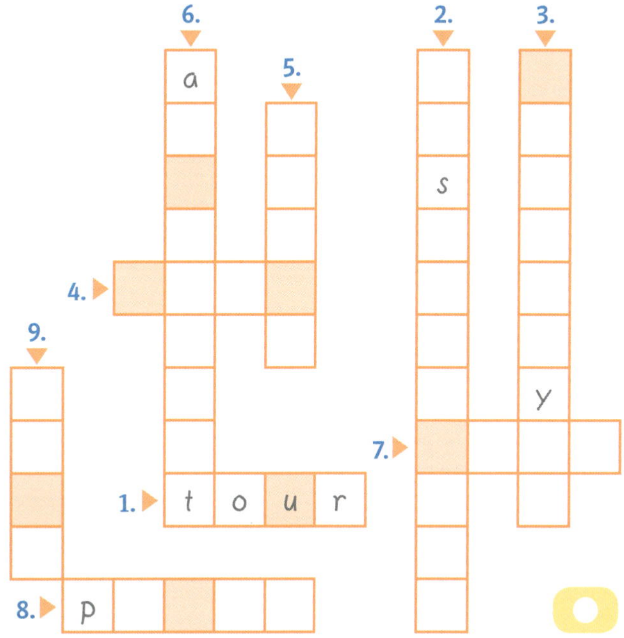

Can you find the the secret word?

c______ ______

77/3a)

2 Make words and sort them into the table.

1. horr	ar
2. cat	sting
3. fascin	ny
4. informa	ible
5. unapp	ating
6. spec	chy
7. bor	ealing
8. intere	ial
9. cle	ing
10. fun	tive

👍	👎
catchy	

77/3b)

3 Find words with almost the same meanings for the underlined words.

1. This ad is amazing; it's really ______________ .
2. I think this ad is boring; it's really ______________ .
3. Nobody needs an ad for tissues; that's silly and ______________ .
4. This ad is really strange; it's very ______________ .

4 (LISTENING) Ads

9
77/4

a) Listen to the radio ads. Which ad is for which picture? Put in the right letter.

Ad 1	Ad 2	Ad 3

10

b) Listen to Daniel and Emily. Complete the sentences.

1. Emily has just seen a ____________________ .
2. Daniel thinks the picture is ________________ .
3. Emily thinks the picture is catchy because of the dog and ______________________ .
4. The slogan says: This lemonade is for ____________________ .
5. Daniel thinks the ________________ is a bit silly but also catchy.
6. Love Lemonade is not a very clear ________________ .

5 What are Emily and Daniel doing? Write sentences in the present progressive.

78/6

climb

read

eat

surf

swim

1. Emily is climbing.
2. Daniel
3. ______________________________
4. ______________________________
5. ______________________________

6 Find the signal words for the simple present and the present progressive.

78/7a)

Circle the signal words for the simple present in blue and the words for the present progressive in red.

never	every …	usually	now	always
often	at the moment	today	sometimes	just

7 Simple present or present progressive?

98/7

a) Put in the right forms

1. It's eight o'clock in the morning and Emily has just woken up. She usually *sleeps* (sleep) in her bedroom, but today she *is sleeping* (sleep) in a tent.
2. Her dog always __________ (eat) its dog food, but at the moment it __________ (run) around.
3. Her dad usually __________ (make) breakfast, but now he __________ (start) a fire.
4. Her mom always __________ (go) to work at eight o'clock, but now she __________ (sleep) in her tent.
5. Her brothers often __________ (stay) in bed late, but today they __________ (collect) wood.
6. Her cat usually __________ (sleep) on her clothes, but today it __________ (sit) on the sofa at home.

b) Write three more sentences about Emily and her family.

get up • stay in tent | write text messages • read book | watch TV • go rock climbing

1. *Her mom usually gets up early, but now she is* __________
2. __________
3. __________

8 Adjective or adverb? Put a circle around the right form.

79/8

1. This meal is deliciously • delicious.
2. They want to feel good • well.
3. The weather in California is often sunny • sunnily.
4. Tourists often sit happy • happily on the beach.
5. Life in California seems easy • easily.
6. Silicon Valley developed quick • quickly.
7. Rock climbing can be very dangerous • dangerously.
8. The view at the top of the mountains looks beautiful • beautifully.

1 What are Linda and Derek saying? Put in the right words.

81/4

tutorials | online | Social media | communicate | trendy | sites | clips | latest | outdated | smartphone | tablet

I watch everything online ______ because TV programs are so boring and ______ . I only use TV to stream movies from my ______ . I also like watching funny video ______ or make-up ______ .

I couldn't live without my ______ . ______ ______ is a part of my life. I ______ with my friends all the time. I check out new ______ a lot to see what's cool and ______ and I watch the ______ news online.

2 Find the right words.

81/5a)

a) Write the words for the symbols.

______ ______ ______ ______ ______

81/5b)

b) Complete the sentences.

1. When something becomes very popular on the internet, it is ______ .
2. When you ______ to a site, you will get emails with information and ads from this site.
3. Hollywood stars often have millions of ______ on social media.

3 (LISTENING) Listen to the school radio. Answer the questions.

11
81/5

1. Why did Kelly stay at home? ______
2. What did Kelly and her friend do after school? Write two things.

______

______

3. What did the principal give Kelly? ______
4. Where did the principal see the photos? ______

82/7

4 What has Linda already done? What hasn't she done yet?

1. *She has already looked at Derek's pictures.*
2. *She hasn't answered Kelly's request yet.*
3. ____________________
4. ____________________
5. ____________________
6. ____________________
7. ____________________
8. ____________________

look at Derek's pictures ✓
answer Kelly's request
share a new website ✓
do homework
read her favourite blog
read her mom's post ✓
open a new email account
watch a funny video clip ✓

82/8a)

5 Complete Linda's blog entry with for or since.

INTERNET ×

What's Cooking?

Welcome to my blog! I'm Linda Wright and I live in San Francisco. I've lived here ________ five years; before that I lived in New York. I go to Saranap High School, and have been there ________ 2014. My favourite subject is Math and ________ the beginning of this year I've been part of the cheerleading squad. I've wanted to join the cheerleaders ________ years. I also play the drums and I've been in the school orchestra ________ two years now. At home I like to cook. I've made our Sunday family lunch every week ________ I was twelve years old. On this blog I'm going to write about new recipes I've tried and want to share. I haven't posted many photos here yet because I've only had this account ________ last week!

82/8b)

6 (YOUR TURN) Write four sentences about yourself. Use for or since.

I have had my own computer since … | I have lived here for … | Since 2011 I have … | Since I was … years old, I have … | I have been in the … club for … | …

1. *I have had my own computer since*
2. ____________________
3. ____________________
4. ____________________

7 Simple past or present perfect?

83/9a)

a) Underline the signal words.

b) Put in the right forms.

1. A century ago people looked (look) at the clock tower to know the time. I 've just checked (check) the time on my phone.
2. I ______ (not watch) TV since 2014. One hundred years ago people only ______ (have) a radio at home.
3. Fifty years ago people ______ (make) friends at sports clubs or in school. I ______ already ______ (find) over 100 friends on social media.
4. Last week I ______ (read) that lots of people don't buy books. People read online. In the 19th and 20th century a lot of people ______ (have) a lot of books in their houses.
5. I ______ just ______ (see) a video clip of a car which could drive itself. In 1900 cars ______ (need) drivers with special training.
6. I ______ (write) a letter since I was ten. Twenty years ago people ______ (send) letters all the time because not everyone had a computer.

8 (WRITING) Write about a new trend.

83/10

a) Choose a trend which you find interesting. You can look for new trends in magazines or on the internet, for example for music and fashion.

b) Write about your trend:

1. Where did you find out about it?
2. Describe the trend.
3. Where is the trend popular?
4. What do you like about the trend?
5. What don't you like about the trend?

I have just found out about a new trend in ______

You can put a picture here.

c) Compare the trends in your group. Which trend is the most interesting?

1 (SPEAKING) Talk about these ads.

83/10

a) Work in groups and talk about the two ads. What do you like about the ads? What don't you like?

I think the layout / design is … | catchy | fascinating | (un)appealing
The headline / slogan is … | (not) informative | clear | boring
The message of the ad is … | I like / I don't like | funny | …

b) Decide in your group which ad you like best.

c) Find two more ads in magazines or on the internet and talk about them.

2 (SPEAKING) Talk about new trends.

83/10

Work in groups of three. Read the information about the new trends. Talk about them in your group.

Glow-in-the-dark hair

The latest hair trend is Phoenix Hair. During the day the hair has a standard neon look but by night it glows in the dark.

Eating insects

Insects are healthy, cheap and tasty. A lot of people eat insects, for example in China. Several restaurants in the USA have them on the menu too.

Trainers which change color

These trainers are the latest thing. You can change their color with an app on your smartphone.

I like / don't like this trend. | I think this trend is … | outdated / out of fashion / …
I would try / buy / … | latest thing / in fashion / … | cool / boring / awful / …

87/5

1 (READING) Read the story.

The mystery of the JOKE gold

Dean looked at the gold. It was the coolest thing he had seen on the trip to the local museum. "Come on, Dean!" said Mrs Donaldson, his history teacher. "Now class, ask your parents or grandparents if someone from your family came to California during the Gold Rush."

"Yes, someone from our family moved here during the Gold Rush," said Dean's dad that night. "He didn't stay here long, just a few years. Then his family moved away again. I moved back here when I met your mother. Why don't you look in the old box in the garage? It's full of old things. You never know: there could be some old photos in there."

Dean opened the box. "What a lot of old things," he thought. Then in the corner he saw a small, red book. It said 'Ken's diary'. He felt excited. "Cool!" he thought and began to read…

24th January 1873
Joe and I played near Mr. Craig's farm last night. There were about five or six men outside. They had a big argument. One of them said, "Why did you throw it in the river? We'll never find it again!" And then another one said, "He'll kill us all when he finds out that it's gone!" Joe and I ran home. This morning everyone talked about a huge piece of gold which Adam Gantry had found. Someone had stolen it from him before he could take it to the bank. Adam says he's going to kill the man who stole it.

25th January 1873
Joe wants to look for the gold! He says we have to do it today or the men will go back for it. It could be anywhere, but we think it's probably somewhere in the river under the bridge. We're going when it's dark.

26th January 1873
I'm so happy! We've found the gold! Joe took his knife and scratched the word 'JOKE' into it, for Joe and Ken Edwards. We've buried it near the station, and we'll wait until everyone has forgotten about Adam and his gold. Then we'll sell it!

30th January 1873
Adam Gantry is really angry. Joe and I are in so much trouble. What are we going to do? We're so scared!

31st January 1873
We've told Pa and we are all leaving town. It's too dangerous to get the gold now. Joe is furious. He says he'll come back some day and get it!

Dean put down the diary. He was excited and couldn't wait to tell his dad about the diary.

2 Guess the German word.

87/5

1. if (line 4) ______________
2. garage (line 10) ______________
3. bank (line 19) ______________
4. to scratch (line 26) ______________
5. bury (line 27) ______________
6. Pa (line 33) ______________

3 Tick the right box.

87/5

	right	wrong
1. Dean saw the JOKE gold at the local museum.	☐	☐
2. Someone from Dean's family moved to California during the Gold Rush.	☐	☐
3. Ken and Joe heard about the gold at school.	☐	☐
4. They thought the gold was in the river.	☐	☐
5. They scratched the first letters of their names on the gold.	☐	☐
6. Adam Gantry wanted his gold back and called the police.	☐	☐
7. Ken and Joe ran away without their dad.	☐	☐
8. They couldn't take the gold with them.	☐	☐

4 How do the people feel in the story? Find the information in the text and complete the sentences.

87/5

1. When Dean finds the diary, he feels ______________ .
2. When Ken and Joe find the gold, they are ______________ .
3. Adam Gantry is really ______________ .
4. Ken and Joe leave town with their dad because they are ______________ .
5. Joe is ______________ because they can't take the gold with them.

5 (WRITING) Why don't Ken and Joe go back for the gold?

87/5

Ken and Joe never went back for the gold. Why didn't they? What do you think? Write two sentences. Here are some ideas to help you:

couldn't find it | scared of Gantry | Pa said no | ...

I think ____

____

____

INTERNET

So darf man als Jugendlicher arbeiten

Die Beschäftigung von Kindern (unter 15 Jahren) und Jugendlichen (ab 15 Jahren), die noch zur Schule gehen, ist in Deutschland grundsätzlich verboten. Es gibt jedoch einige Ausnahmen, die Aushilfs- und Ferienjobs ermöglichen.

Kinder ab dem 13. Lebensjahr und Jugendliche, die noch zur Schule gehen, dürfen mit Einwilligung der Eltern stundenweise beschäftigt werden, soweit die Beschäftigung leicht und für sie geeignet ist. Erlaubt sind z. B.:

- → das Austragen von Zeitungen, Zeitschriften, Prospekten etc.
- → Tätigkeiten in Haushalt, Garten und Landwirtschaft
- → Botengänge
- → Betreuung von Kindern oder Haustieren
- → Nachhilfeunterricht
- → Tätigkeiten bei Veranstaltungen von Kirchen, Verbänden und Vereinen.

Die Arbeitszeit darf nicht mehr als zwei Stunden täglich, in der Landwirtschaft nicht mehr als drei Stunden täglich betragen. Außerdem dürfen die Jugendlichen nicht zwischen 6 Uhr abends und 8 Uhr morgens und nicht vor oder während des Schulunterrichts arbeiten. An Samstagen, Sonntagen und Feiertagen darf ebenfalls nicht gearbeitet werden.

Während der Schulferien können Jugendliche einen Ferienjob von höchstens vier Wochen Dauer ausüben. Die maximale Arbeitszeit darf acht Stunden täglich und 40 Stunden wöchentlich nicht überschreiten.

88/2

1 (MEDIATION) Read the text and answer the questions in English.

1. What is the minimum age for teenagers who want to get a job?

____

2. Write three examples of jobs which teenagers are allowed to do.

____

____

3. When are teenagers allowed to work?

____

____

____

4. What does the text say about jobs during the holidays?

____

____

____

Ziel 1: Ich kann Informationen über Kalifornien und den Westen der USA verstehen.

The history of Hollywood

Hollywood has a lot of movie studios, theaters and it's where all the most important stars live. Millions of tourists go to Hollywood every year, over 5,000 every day. They visit movie studios and hope to see their favorite star on the streets. But how did Hollywood become so famous? About a hundred years ago, the USA became richer and richer. People had more money than ever before and wanted to spend it in their free time. Going to the movies became almost everyone's favorite hobby! In the 1920s movies were still silent, but after 1927 more and more movies had sound. A lot of movie studios moved to Hollywood because of the dry, warm weather, which made it easier to film outside.
The Hollywood sign was built in 1923. It was an ad for the houses which were built in the Hollywood Hills. Today it is one of the most famous sights in the USA.

Read the text and answer the questions.

1. How many tourists visit Hollywood every day?

____

2. Why did people go to the movies in the 1920s?

____

____

3. Why did movie studios move to Hollywood?

____

4. Why did people put up the Hollywood sign in 1923?

____

4P

→ p. 72/1

Ziel 2: Ich kann eine Werbeanzeige gestalten.

_______________ _______________ _______________

_______________ _______________ _______________

Design an ad for a surf club called Super Surf Club. Choose one of the pictures and think of a good slogan. Write the slogan under the picture.

friends	everyone	have fun	enjoy
surf	learn	meet	waves

3P

→ p. 72/2

Ziel 3: Ich kann über Trends sprechen.

What do you think of this trend? Complete the dialogue.

New ice-cream maker

Making your own ice cream is easier than you think. You can use anything you like - fresh fruit, chocolate or nuts. You can also try something new and make ice cream that isn't sweet. Try ice cream with tomato, salt and pepper or ham and cheese.

Your friends will love it!

Your friend:	Hey, have you heard about this new ice-cream maker? What do you think of it?
You:	I think ______________________
Your friend:	Have you ever made your own ice cream?
You:	______________________ I think the machine is ______________
	I would ____________ it.
Your friend:	I could eat ice cream every day. What kind of ice cream would you make with it?
You:	____
Your friend:	Would you make ice cream with vegetables or cheese?
You:	____

6P

→ p. 73/3

Ziel 4: Ich kann einen Text über den Goldrausch verstehen.

Read the text on page 66 of your workbook again. Put the sentences in the right order.

- [1] Dean goes on a trip to the local museum.
- [ ] Joe and Ken find the gold. The scratch the word 'JOKE' into it.
- [ ] Dean finds Ken's diary in an old box. He reads the diary.
- [ ] Ken, Joe and Pa leave town because they are scared.
- [ ] Dean's dad talks about their family during the Gold Rush.
- [ ] They bury the gold near the station.
- [ ] Dean wants to tell his dad about the diary.
- [ ] First he reads about Adam Gantry. Gantry was angry because he lost a big piece of gold.

7P

→ p. 73/4

Ziel 5: Ich kann Informationen über Kinderarbeit weitergeben.

Children working on a construction site

Police are interviewing the boss of a construction site in Los Angeles because people reported that they had seen children there. Someone even sent a video to the police, which was filmed in secret on a phone. It shows twelve-year-old children who are working on the construction site. They are carrying heavy boxes and even driving a truck.

Our reporter talked to the boss of the construction site. He said, "The children didn't get any money. Their parents work on the construction site and the children just wanted to join them. I didn't do anything wrong."

Children under 14 aren't allowed to work on a construction site because the work is too dangerous and it doesn't matter if they get paid or not.

a) Lies den Text und beantworte die Fragen auf Deutsch.

1. In welcher Stadt war die Baustelle? ______
2. Wie hat die Polizei davon erfahren? ______
3. Was sagt der Eigentümer der Baustelle dazu? ______
4. Dürfen Kinder unter 14 auf Baustellen arbeiten? ______

b) Complete the dialogue on the telephone.

Job Center: Hello, this is the LA Job Center. What can I do for you today?

You: (sage, dass du einen Teilzeitjob während der Sommerferien suchst)

______

Job Center: OK. How old are you?

You: (sage, dass du 15 Jahre alt bist und frage, welche Jobs du machen darfst)

______

Job Center: You can babysit or work in a house. During your holidays you can also work on a farm.

You: (frage, wie man einen Job auf einem Bauernhof findet)

______

Job Center: You can look on our website.

You: (bedanke dich für die Hilfe)

______

8P

→ p. 73/5

Lösungen online
5z29zc

○ **Ziel 1: Ich kann Informationen über Kalifornien und den Westen der USA verstehen.**

California is on the West Coast of the USA. The capital of California is Sacramento but the most famous cities in the state are Los Angeles and San Francisco. A lot of tourists travel to these two cities every year and visit Hollywood, the Walk of Fame or the Golden Gate Bridge.

California is also famous for its relaxed outdoor lifestyle. People enjoy beach sports or go hiking or camping. Silicon Valley is famous for its modern high-tech companies. California's nickname is 'The Golden State' because of the Gold Rush which started in 1849. At that time thousands of people moved West to look for gold.

Complete the sentences.

1. California is a state on the ______________ of the USA.
2. The capital of California is ______________ .
3. ______________ visit Hollywood, the Walk of Fame or the Golden Gate Bridge.
4. People in California enjoy ______________ .
5. ______________ is famous for its high-tech companies.
6. At the time of ______________ , thousands of people moved to the west to look for gold.

○ **Ziel 2: Ich kann eine Werbeanzeige gestalten.**

Choose slogans for the ads below.

Climbing is cool.

Sun, fun, surfing!

Big trees, big mountains, great adventure!

Good food, happy life.

____

____

____

____

○ **Ziel 3: Ich kann über Trends sprechen.**

Use the words to write a dialogue.

I think it's interesting. | I think it's silly. | No, I wouldn't buy it. | Yes, I would like to try it. | I would make ice cream with … | Yes, I would. / No, I wouldn't.

Your friend: Hey, what do you think of the new tomato ice cream?
You: ______
Your friend: Would you buy it?
You: ______
Your friend: I could eat ice cream every day. What kind of ice cream would you make?
You: ______
Your friend: Would you buy ice cream with ham and cheese?
You: ______

○ **Ziel 4: Ich kann einen Text über den Goldrausch verstehen.**

Read the text on pages 84–86 in your book again. Complete the sentences.

1. In 1848 the President of the United States confirmed the discovery of ______ in California.
2. Men stopped working and moved ______ .
3. Edward wanted to give up but then he thought about his wife and his ______ .
4. He found a little ______ of gold.
5. The gold ______ did not last long.

○ **Ziel 5: Ich kann Informationen über Kinderarbeit weitergeben.**

Many new factories were built in the USA at the end of the 19th century. By 1900 about 1.7 million children under the age of 16 worked in these factories. Children were useful because they were small and fast and could get under and on top of the big machines. They were also cheap to pay. Of course this work was very dangerous, and children often got hurt. These conditions changed in 1938. The new rules protected children from difficult and dangerous work.

1. Wie viele Kinder arbeiteten um 1900 in den Fabriken?
   ______
2. Wie alt waren die Kinder?
   ______
3. Warum wurden Kinder beschäftigt?
   ______
   ______
4. Wann gab es ein neues Gesetz zur Kinderarbeit?
   ______

95/3

1 Collect sentences and questions you need for an interview. Complete the table.

Asking about someone's name, age, town and family	What's your name? Where
Asking about school / job	Do you go
Asking about hobbies and free time	
Asking about an interesting / unusual fact or situation	Tell me Have you ever
Showing an interest	I can imagine
Sounding surprised	Wow,
Saying thank you	

Schau dir nochmal die Sätze in deinem Buch auf Seite 94 an. Du kannst dir auch eigene Sätze überlegen.

95/3

2 Read the role cards.

Name: Taylor Spence
Age: 16
Lives in: Los Angeles, California

Personal information:
- likes watching car races and playing computer games
- has a dog called Jimbo
- part-time job on the weekends (sells drinks at the football stadium)

Interesting fact:
once took his dad's car; had an accident; saves money from his job to repair his dad's car

Name: Alison James
Age: 15
Lives in: San Francisco, California

Personal information:
- likes singing, going to the movies and hanging out with friends
- has two sisters
- doesn't have any pets
- doesn't have a part-time job

Interesting fact:
was in a singing competition; won first place and $1,000 dollars

95/3

3 Do an interview.

a) Work with a partner. Choose one of the role cards. You are the person on the role card. Your partner interviews you.

b) Now your partner chooses the other role card. Interview your partner.

95/3

4 Make your own role card and act another interview.

Name: ______________________________

Age: ______________________________

Lives in: ______________________________

Personal information:

____

____

____

Interesting fact:

____

____

____

____

INTERNET ×

CCC (Coffee, Cake, Cats!)

Welcome to CCC! This is the first cat café in Sacramento, California. Visit us for delicious food and drinks, and meet our lovely friendly workers, our cats! We are in Irvine and are open every day from 8 a.m. to 5 p.m.

Meet our cats

At the moment there are 20 cats at CCC. The number changes every few weeks because our cats come from animal shelters. Our customers can then take a cat home as a pet. We have baby cats and older cats. At the moment our youngest cat is Julius. He is four months old, and our oldest cat is Martha. She's twelve! All our cats are nice.

How does it work?

Our café has two rooms – one is for food and drinks, where you can enjoy our cake and coffee. You can buy souvenirs here too, like T-shirts and pens. The other room is our 'cat playroom'. You can spend up to an hour there and play with the cats.

Dos and Don'ts

These are our rules:

- Make a reservation. Call or send us an email. If you don't have a reservation, you will have to wait.
- Children under twelve must bring an adult.
- Please don't feed the cats.
- You can take photos of the cats but please be careful. Don't scare the cats.

A READING

1 What can you do at the cat café? Tick the right boxes.

1. Find a pet. ☐
2. Feed the cats. ☐
3. Buy souvenirs. ☐
4. Come without an adult if you are under twelve. ☐
5. Take photos. ☐
6. Enjoy coffee and cake. ☐

2 Answer the questions.

1. Where is the cat café? ______
2. How many cats are there at the moment? ______
3. Where do the cats come from? ______
4. How can you make a reservation? ______
5. Can children under twelve visit the café? ______

B LISTENING

12 **3 Listen to the radio ads. Which ad is for which picture? Write the number under the picture.**

A

______

B

______

C

______

12 **4 Listen again and tick the right box.**

	right	wrong
1. You can meet new people at Sam's Gym.	☐	☐
2. Sports isn't fun at Sam's Gym.	☐	☐
3. You can get free make-up on Saturday.	☐	☐
4. There is a special sale at the department store this month.	☐	☐
5. Perfect Pets is open every day.	☐	☐
6. It's the biggest pet store in New York.	☐	☐

Unit 5

Southern life

13 97/3

1 (LISTENING) Listen to the radio report about the South.

a) Put the pictures in the right order.

b) Listen again. Then write one title for each picture.

97/3

2 Find the information on the internet.

1. Name six US states which belong to the South.

2. What is the biggest state in the South? ____________

3. Name two famous leaders of the American Civil Rights Movement.

4. Name two Southern dishes. ____________

5. Who was Louis Armstrong? ____________

98/1

1 Put in the right words.

fry | influences | chicken | follow | dish ✓ | oil | multicultural

Jambalaya is a popular __________ from New Orleans. It is made with rice, meat and vegetables. Jambalaya has French and Spanish __________, so this dish shows how __________ the city is. To make the dish, __________ this recipe. First, __________ the vegetables in __________, then add meat, such as __________ or sausage. Finally, add rice, water and spices and cook for 30 minutes.

99/3a)

2 Write the countries and nationalities.

1.  China / Chinese
2.  __________ / __________
3.  __________ / __________
4.  __________ / __________
5.  __________ / __________
6.  __________ / __________

3 Find the right words about conflicts and solutions.

99/4a)

a) Put in the right words.

agree ✓ | tolerate | ban | disagree | accept | protest

1. The opposite of disagree is agree.
2. When people don't like something, they can __________ against it.
3. When you have a different opinion, you __________.
4. A lot of people think that the government should __________ the Confederate flag.
5. Nobody should __________ discrimination.
6. In the 1950s there were protests because people didn't __________ discrimination.

99/4b)

b) Find words for the definitions.

1. When you find something good, you __________ it.
2. When you don't want something, you __________ it.
3. When you think someone is a great person, you __________ them.

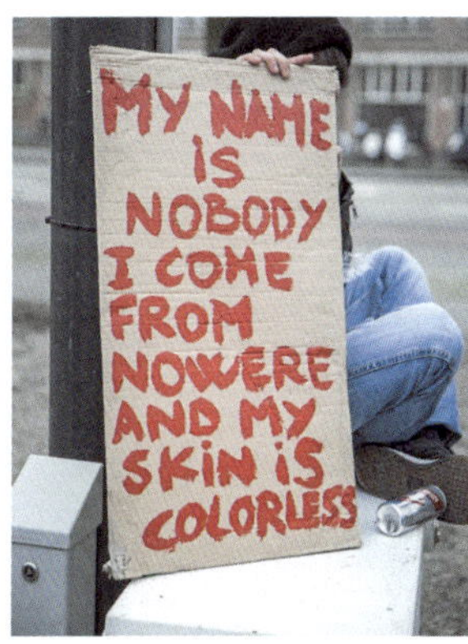

14
99/4

4 (LISTENING) Listen to Sam. He is talking about his family. Answer the questions.

1. Where does Sam's mom come from?
   ____
2. Where did Sam's parents meet?
   ____
3. What does Sam's dad's grandfather like to tell?
   ____
4. Who is Native American in his family? ______________________
5. What is his aunt's job? ______________________
6. Finish the sentence. There is no racism in ______________________

100/5

5 Choose is or are.

1. Spanish *is* spoken in Mexico.
2. Jazz music ________ played at the Mardi Gras Carnival.
3. A lot of tourists ________ attracted to the South.
4. The Confederate flag ________ not tolerated any more.
5. Soybeans and corn ________ grown on farms in the South.
6. Souvenirs ________ sold in New Orleans.
7. Fried chicken ________ made a lot in Southern states.
8. Spices ________ often put in fried chicken.

100/6

6 Put in the passive form.

Fried chicken is *eaten* (eat) in the American South. This dish is ________ (make) with chicken, spices and flour. Spices are ________ (put) into a lot of dishes. Rice is often ________ (mix) with beans. Soups are often ________ (cook) with potatoes and corn. Tea is ________ (serve) cold. It is ________ (drink) at breakfast, lunch and dinner. Barbecues are ________ (enjoy) all the time.

Achte auf unregelmäßige Verbformen. Schau auf Seite 216 im Buch nach. Dort findest du alle unregelmäßigen Verben aufgelistet. Du brauchst die Form in der dritten Spalte.

00/7a)

7 Make passive sentences in the simple present.

1. A lot of American movies _are shown_ (show) in German cinemas.
2. A lot of tourists ______________ (attract) to the American South.
3. Soybeans ______________ (grow) by farms in the South.
4. A peaceful protest ______________ (accept) by the US government.
5. Lots of languages ______________ (speak) by immigrants in the USA.
6. The Confederate flag ______________ (tolerate) by some people in the South.
7. Lots of cultures ______________ (bring) to the USA by immigrants.
8. Dishes from many different countries ______________ (eat) by people in the South.

01/8a)

8 Make passive sentences in the simple past.

1. Nashville _was founded_ (found) in 1779.
2. A place near a river ______________ (choose) as the location for the city.
3. The city ______________ (name) after Francis Nash, an American hero.
4. It ______________ (call) the 'Music City' by a DJ in 1950.
5. The country music industry ______________ (develop) in the city in the 1950s.
6. Nashville's first skyscraper ______________ (build) in 1957.
7. The Music City Center ______________ (open) in 2013.

101/9

9 (YOUR TURN) Write a text about the different cultures where you live.

The words in the boxes can help you to write your text.

shops	signs	You can buy ...	Turkish	Greek	Chinese
restaurants	music	You can hear ...	Spanish	Italian	Russian
languages	multicultural	You can see ...	Portuguese	...	

I live in ______________________________

____

____

____

____

____

____

____

____

102/2

1 Find the right nouns.

1. to pack → package
2. to book → ______
3. to pick up → ______
4. to turn → ______
5. to choose → ______
6. to show → ______
7. to sit → ______
8. hot → ______

15
103/4

2 (LISTENING) Listen to the telephone call.

Write the information.

Everglades Tours

- Date: Saturday the 13th
- Number of people: ______
- Time trip starts: ______
- Hotel: ______
- Pick-up time: ______
- Price: ______
- Animals in wildlife show: ______

3 Complete the dialogues.

103/5a)

a) What can you say in these situations?

Linda: I'd love to see a baby alligator in the Everglades.
Robert: I'm sorry, but I ______
Linda: I said that I'd love to see a baby alligator.

Robert: Those jungle trails sound cool but I'm a bit scared of the snakes.
Jake: Oh yes, ______

Jake: I'd like to watch a NASCAR race.
Linda: Could ______ what NASCAR is?
Jake: NASCAR is a car race.

103/5b)

b) Write dialogues in your exercise book with these words.

Please repeat that. **Absolutely!** **What do you mean by '...'?**

104/7

4 Report what Linda, Jake and Robert say during their trip.

1. Linda: "I feel sick."
2. Jake: "I'm not scared of snakes."
3. Robert and Linda: "We have a great view."
4. Robert: "I can see an alligator!"
5. Jake and Robert: "We're looking forward to the jungle trail."
6. Linda: "I don't like insects."
7. Jake: "I need something to drink."

Pronomen und Verben ändern sich in der indirekten Rede:
I → he / she
I love → he / she loves
we → they

1. Linda says that she feels sick.
2. Jake says that he isn't scared of snakes.
3. ______
4. ______
5. ______
6. ______
7. ______

104/8

5 Jake knows a lot about animals. Report what the others ask him.

Robert:
1. How much do alligators weigh?
2. Where do alligators sleep?
3. How many teeth do alligators have?
4. How fast can alligators run?

Linda:
5. What do snakes eat?
6. How long do snakes live?
7. When do snakes sleep?

How much ~~do~~ alligators weigh?
Robert asks how much alligators weigh.

1. Robert asks how much alligators weigh.
2. ______
3. ______
4. ______
5. ______
6. ______
7. ______

6 Report what the animal trainer said about alligators.

105/9a)

Alligators grow to about four meters long. They are black or dark brown with white on their stomachs. They sometimes live to be 80 years old! Alligators only live in the USA and China. They eat fish and birds. They don't usually attack people. Some people eat alligator meat.

Achte auf die Zeitverschiebung:
"They grow to about four meters long."
→ He said (that) they grew to about four meters long.

The animal trainer said that alligators grew to about four meters long. He said that

____

____

____

____

____

____

____

7 Report what people at the NASCAR race said.

105/9b)

Man:
1. It is the most important race of the season.
2. My cousin is the driver of the blue car.
3. We have great seats this time.

Woman:
4. I prefer bike races.
5. It's very noisy.
6. The race looks really dangerous.

1. *The man said that it was the most important race of the season.*
2. ______________________________
3. ______________________________
4. ______________________________
5. ______________________________
6. ______________________________

105/10

1 (SPEAKING) What should people do in these situations?

a) Read the four texts. What would you do in these situations? Discuss your ideas in your group.

There is a new student in your class. Some students think his clothes look strange and they laugh at him.

You are in a café with your friends. There is a sign on the door which says, "No dogs, please." A girl with a dog comes in and sits down at the table next to you.

Your friend is 16. He wants a new pair of jeans. He doesn't have the money for them and wants to get a job. There is a job ad for a night club but you have to be 18 to work there. He wants to go to the club and tell them he is already 18.

You have new neighbors. Every Saturday night they have a party and play loud music. You and your parents can't sleep.

These words can help you discuss your ideas:

- I would help / talk to the boy.
- I would ask the girl with the dog to …
- I would tell my friend that it is wrong.
- I would go talk to my neighbors and …
- I would tell them to stop it.
- I agree / I disagree
- I think / I don't think
- I would try to …
- …

b) Think of one more situation. Discuss it in your group.

1 (READING) Read the story about Mr. Washington.

107/5

An interesting neighbor

It was a long, hot summer vacation. Most of my friends had gone away with their parents, and my mom and dad were busy with work. I was bored, so I made some ads and put them in my neighbors' mailboxes[1]. I said I could do work in gardens and around the house.

My first call was from Mr. Washington. He was an old man in his 80s who lived around the corner and needed someone to mow[2] his big lawn[3]. I went to do it the next day. It was a very hot day and it was hard work. When I had finished, I went to see Mr. Washington.

"Come on up, Brad," Mr. Washington said. "You've done a good job. Here, have a glass of lemonade." He pulled out a chair for me. The cold drink was great.
"Thank you, sir," I said. "It really is hot out there."
"Yeah, it's a hot summer," he answered. "My parents were out in this kind of weather all day in the cotton fields."
"Cotton fields?" I was surprised. "But your parents weren't slaves!"
"No they weren't," said Mr. Washington. "But my family worked in the cotton fields for many generations. There were no more slaves, but we still worked in the cotton fields."
"Were things really that bad?" I asked.

"Oh, yes. For black people anyway. A lot of white people were scared. They thought black people would be angry after all those years of slavery[4]. So, you know, black and white people had to be separate. Separate schools, hospitals, bathrooms, separate seats in restaurants and cinemas. They didn't want to see that we were human too. So, my parents worked hard in the fields and we went to school, but it wasn't a very good school. The Black schools did not have a lot of money."

Mr. Washington looked sad. "And we fought, my sisters and I. My parents said it was dangerous, but we joined the Civil Rights Movement and protested. We had had enough. And then my sisters and I went to university and we found good jobs."

He laughed. Suddenly we were back in the present.
"And you know what? My mom and dad would not believe that a white kid from a nice family just mowed my lawn." He put some money in my hand. "Life is funny, isn't it? Same time next week?"
"Sure, Mr. Washington. Thank you. And thanks for the lemonade."

I left his house. Yes, I thought, it was funny. I had mowed a lawn, and this job had had a lot of meaning.

1 mailbox ['meɪlbɒks] – *Briefkasten;* 2 to mow [məʊ] – *mähen;* 3 lawn [lɔːn] – *Rasen;* 4 slavery ['sleɪvri] – *Sklaverei*

107/5

2 Where in the story can you find the information?

Line(s) in the story.

1. Brad's vacation was not very interesting. __________
2. Garden work could be difficult. __________
3. The weather was very hot. __________
4. Mr. Washington's family worked in the cotton fields. __________
5. There were separate places for black and white people. __________
6. Mr. Washington and his sisters protested. __________
7. Mr. Washington paid Brad for his work. __________

107/5

3 Complete the table.

Sort the facts in the boxes about Mr. Washington and Brad. Which facts are about Mr. Washingon? Which facts are about Brad? Write the facts in the table.

on vacation	has a house with a big garden	was bored
in his 80s ✓	his parents were busy	parents worked in the fields
protested	has sisters	went to university
is a student	wanted a summer job	learned some history

Mr. Washington	Brad
in his 80s	

107/5

4 Write about Brad or Mr. Washington.

Use the information in exercise 3 and the story to write about Brad or Mr. Washington.

INTERNET ×

Culture in the South

The people of the Southern states of the USA are famous around the country and the world for being friendly. Family and the church are very important in most people's lives.

You should always remember to respect older people. It is polite to call them 'sir' and 'ma'am'. People in the South also have very good manners so it is important to remember to always say 'please' and 'thank you' and greet people with 'Hello' or 'How are you?' Other important things you should do is to always show respect to the American flag and to remember to take off your hat when you meet someone or walk into a building. Also, people do not usually kiss when they meet; they normally offer their hand instead. And don't forget: if you are invited to someone's house, bring a small present like flowers or something to eat.

108/2

1 (MEDIATION) **Worauf sollte man achten, wenn man den Süden der USA besucht? Fasse die wichtigsten Punkte zusammen.**

Man sollte ältere Menschen respektieren und

108/2

2 (MEDIATION) **At a party in Alabama**

Du besuchst Verwandte in Alabama. Ihr geht zu einer Party und du unterhältst dich dort mit einer älteren Dame. Denke daran, sehr höflich zu sein.

Woman: Hello, how are you?
You: (begrüße die Dame und sag, dass es dir gut geht)

Woman: You've got a nice accent. Where do you come from?
You: (sage, dass du sie nicht verstanden hast, und bitte sie, das Gesagte nochmal zu wiederholen)

Woman: Of course. I asked where you came from.
You: (sage, dass du aus Deutschland kommst und dass du Alabama großartig findest)

Woman: Oh, thank you! I'd love to go to Germany one day.

Ziel 1: Ich kann Informationen über die Südstaaten der USA verstehen.

Come to the South!

Come and visit the Southern states of the USA on your next vacation. There is so much to see and do! You can visit wildlife parks, beautiful beaches and swamps in Florida. Or you can take a boat trip along the spectacular Mississippi River. If you love music, you will enjoy a visit to Nashville, the home of country music, or a visit to the festivals and jazz clubs in New Orleans. The region is full of history, from stories of the early immigrants, to the lives of the African Americans who came here as slaves and then influenced the culture of the area. Everywhere you go you can enjoy delicious Southern food.

Answer the questions.

1. What kind of text is this? ______
2. What can you visit in Florida? ______
3. What can you do on the Mississippi River? ______
4. Which cities should people who love music visit? ______
5. What history can you learn there? ______

   ______
6. What can you enjoy everywhere you go? ______

6P

→ p. 92/1

Ziel 2: Ich kann über Einflüsse verschiedener Kulturen im täglichen Leben sprechen.

Read the information. What can you say about the city of Memphis? Write complete sentences.

In the past Native Americans first settled

in the area of Memphis.

______

______

______

______

______

______

______

______

Memphis

- Native Americans first settled in the area
- city founded in 1819
- city's culture influenced by African Americans
- attracts a lot of music stars
- famous for its music
- several music museums located in the city

7P

→ p. 92/2

Ziel 3: Ich kann andere über Freizeitaktivitäten informieren.

On the weekends I usually play football for my local team. I love football. After the game I often have lunch with some friends. In the afternoon I do my homework. In the summer my family and I often go to the beach. In the winter I go to the cinema or hang out with friends at home. I like computer games and action movies.

Report what Robert said about his weekends.

Robert said that he usually played football ________________

7P

→ p. 93/3

Ziel 4: Ich kann einen Bericht über Rassismus verstehen.

Read the text on page 86 again. Put the sentences in the right order.

- [ ] Brad thought about Mr. Washington when he left his house.
- [ ] His first job was in Mr. Washington's garden.
- [ ] Mr. Washington also talked about how there used to be separate schools, hospitals and restaurants for black and white people.
- [ ] When Brad was finished in the garden, Mr. Washington gave him some lemonade and they talked.
- [ ] Mr. Washington paid Brad.
- [ ] Mr. Washington also joined the Civil Rights Movement.
- [1] Brad was bored and wanted a job.
- [ ] Mr. Washington talked about his family and their work in the cotton fields.
- [ ] Brad is going to help Mr. Washington again next week.

9P

→ p. 93/4

Ziel 5: Ich kann Informationen über Rituale weitergeben

Religion plays an important role in the lives of many Americans, especially in the Southern states. Although there is no official US religion and there are people of many different religions (such as people who are Jewish, Muslim, etc) the majority of Americans say they are Christian. Because of this Easter and Christmas are big celebrations. During these holidays most companies are closed and people have some time off work and school to spend with their families.

In the South most people go to church on these holidays, and many people go to church every Sunday too. Religion also plays an important role in the social life of many people. Regular barbecues, sports games and parties are organised by local churches.

a) Lies den Text und beantworte die Fragen auf Deutsch.

1. Welche Religion haben die meisten Menschen in den USA? ______
2. Welche anderen Religionen gibt es in den USA? ______
3. Was sind die wichtigsten christlichen Feiertage? ______
4. Wann gehen viele Menschen im Süden in die Kirche? ______

   ______
5. Warum ist die Kirche noch wichtig? ______

   ______

b) Du bist zu Besuch bei Verwandten im Süden der USA. Auf einer Grillparty unterhältst du dich mit der Gastgeberin und einem anderen deutschen Gast, der nicht so gut Englisch kann. Vermittle.

Guest: Sag ihr bitte danke für die Einladung.

You: *He says* ______

Host: You're welcome. I'm glad you could come. Would you like some coleslaw?

You: ______

______

Guest: Ich weiß nicht. Kannst du sie fragen, was das ist?

You: ______

Host: It's a salad made with cabbage, carrots and mayonnaise.

You: ______

Guest: Sag ihr, dass ich ihn gerne probieren möchte.

You: ______

9P

→ p. 93/5

Lösungen online
qx99hd

Ziel 1: Ich kann Informationen über die Südstaaten der USA verstehen.

There are a lot of exciting things to see and do in the Southern states of the USA. People who enjoy the outdoors can visit mountains, beautiful beaches or swamps.

The South has its own lifestyle with its own customs and culture. Several styles of music started in the South.

In the 18th century African slaves were brought to the South. They had to work on the plantations of the European settlers.

Until the 1950s African Americans in the South had few rights. They had to fight against discrimination.

Read the texts and complete the sentences.

1. There are a lot of ________________ things to see and do in the Southern states of the USA.
2. People who enjoy the outdoors can visit mountains, beaches or ________________ .
3. The South has its own ________________ with its own customs and culture.
4. Several styles of music ________________ in the South.
5. In the 18th century African ________________ had to work on the plantations of the European settlers.
6. African Americans had to fight against ________________ .

Ziel 2: Ich kann über Einflüsse verschiedener Kulturen im täglichen Leben sprechen.

Put in the right words.

one language	other countries	multicultural society ✓
other cultures	language	courses

In a multicultural society people do not accept racism. They welcome people from ________________ . People often speak more than ________________ and in some schools different languages are taught by the teachers. People who don't speak the official ________________ can go to special ________________ . People from other countries often bring their own dishes with them and open restaurants. Everyone can enjoy influences from ________________ .

Ziel 3: Ich kann andere über Freizeitaktivitäten informieren.

Report what these people said about their free time.

Robert

Linda

Jake

I play football every weekend. I like sports and action movies.

I'm very busy right now. I go to school and I have a part-time job.

On the weekends I often visit my dad. He lives in New Orleans.

Robert said that he ____________________

He ____________________

Linda said that ____________________

She ____________________

Jake said that ____________________

He ____________________

Ziel 4: Ich kann einen Bericht über Rassismus verstehen.

Read the text on pages 106–107 in your book again. Choose the right answer.

1. In the 1950s people's lives in the South were	a) segregated.	☐	b) easier.	☐
2. Claudette believed that segregation was	a) fair.	☐	b) unfair.	☐
3. She didn't give up her seat to	a) others.	☐	b) whites.	☐
4. The police came and she was	a) arrested.	☐	b) taken home.	☐
5. Claudette lost a lot of friends because they were	a) angry.	☐	b) afraid.	☐
6. In the end her protest was a	a) success.	☐	b) disaster.	☐

Ziel 5: Ich kann Informationen über Rituale weitergeben.

Religion plays an important role in the lives of many Americans, especially in the Southern states. Although there is no official US religion and there are people of many different religions (such as people who are Jewish, Muslim, etc) the majority of Americans say they are Christian. Because of this Easter and Christmas are big celebrations. During these holidays most companies are closed and people have some time off work and school.

Lies den Text und beantworte die Fragen auf Deutsch.

1. Welche Religion haben die meisten Amerikaner?

____

2. Welche anderen Religionen gibt es in den USA?

____

3. Was sind die wichtigsten christlichen Feiertage?

____

SPEAKING

35/5

Describing a school day

Most students go to school by …	Die meisten Schüler fahren mit … zur Schule.
Then there is …	Dann gibt es …
School starts at …	Die Schule fängt um … an.
After that …	Danach …

41/11

Talking about your job

I work at …	Ich arbeite bei …
I like my job because …	Ich mag meine Arbeit / meinen Job, weil …
I earn …	Ich verdiene …
I work on …	Ich arbeite am …

51/4

Giving a presentation

My presentation is about …	In meiner Präsentation geht es um …
First, I'd like to talk about …	Zuerst möchte ich über … sprechen.
Now I am going to talk about …	Jetzt werde ich über … sprechen.
My next topic is …	Mein nächstes Thema ist …
Second, … . Finally, …	Zweitens … . Schließlich …

55/4a)

Making small talk

How are you doing? / How are you?	Wie geht es dir?
What's new?	Gibt's was Neues?
So what have you been up to?	Was hast du in letzter Zeit gemacht?
How is he / she?	Wie geht es ihm / ihr ?

59/5a); 61/10

Giving your opinion

That's true.	Das ist wahr.
I don't think so.	Das glaube ich nicht.
Exactly.	Genau.
That's for sure.	Das stimmt.
You're right.	Du hast recht.

95/3

Doing an interview

Our guest today is …	Heute ist … unser Gast.
Tell me more …	Erzähl /Erzählen Sie mir mehr …
It was really interesting talking to you.	Es war sehr interessant, mit Ihnen / dir zu reden.
Thanks so much.	Vielen Dank.

103/5a)

Saying you understand or don't understand

I get it.	Ich verstehe (es). / Ich habe verstanden.
I know what you mean.	Ich weiß, was Sie meinen / du meinst.
I see.	Ich verstehe.
I'm sorry, I didn't catch that.	Es tut mir leid, aber das habe ich nicht verstanden.
Excuse me?	Wie bitte?

WRITING

21/9 Writing a magazine article

His / Her name is …	Er / Sie heißt …
He / She is from …	Er / Sie kommt aus …
He / She immigrated to … when …	Er / Sie ist eingewandert nach / in die … als …
His / Her parents were …	Seine / Ihre Eltern waren …
He / She now lives in …	Er / Sie lebt jetzt in …

37/11 Writing a comparison

I would like to compare … and …	Ich möchte gerne … mit … vergleichen.
For … this is the same.	Für … ist es / gilt dasselbe.
But … is different.	Aber … ist anders.
Finally …	Schließlich …

73/3 Writing a summary

The article was written by …	Der Artikel wurde von … geschrieben.
The text is about …	In dem Text geht es um …
It explains / describes …	Er erklärt / beschreibt …
First / Second / Third …	Erstens / Zweitens / Drittens …
Then / After that …	Dann / Danach …
To sum up I can say …	Zusammenfassend kann ich sagen …
In general the article explains …	Im Allgemeinen erklärt der Artikel …
I think …	Ich denke / glaube …
In my opinion …	Meiner Meinung nach …

77/4 Writing about an ad

The headline is funny and …	Die Überschrift ist witzig und …
The message is clear and …	Die Botschaft ist deutlich und …
The layout is boring …	Das Layout ist langweilig …

107/5a) Writing a biography

He / She was born in (*place*) in (*year*).	Er / Sie wurde (*Jahr*) in (*Ort*) geboren.
He / She went to school in …	Er / Sie ging in … zur Schule.
He / She fought for …	Er / Sie kämpfte um / für …
He / She fought against …	Er / Sie kämpfte gegen …
He / She invented …	Er / Sie erfand …
He / She was famous for …	Er / Sie war berühmt für …
He / She died in (*place*) in (*year*).	Er / Sie starb (*Jahr*) in (*Ort*).

107/5b) Giving an opinion

I agree with …	Ich stimme … zu.
I disagree with …	Ich stimme … nicht zu.
In my opinion …	Meiner Meinung nach …
According to …	… zufolge … / Gemäß …
On the one hand …	Einerseits …
On the other hand …	Andererseits …

Audios zum Hörverstehen

Aufnahmeleitung: Ernst Klett Verlag
Redaktion: Lisa Poeira
Sprecherinnen und Sprecher: Eva Alexander, Ethan Brooke, Peter Brooke, John Chancer, DeNica Fairman, Walles Hammonde, John Hasler, Helen Johns, Jules de Jongh, David Menkin, Rhonda Miller, Heather Nichol, Christopher Ragland, Patricia Rodriguez, Caitlin Shannon, Martin S. Sherman

Produktion: John Green, TEFL Audio, London
Tontechnik: Tim Woolf
Gesamtzeit: 26' 49''

Inhaltsverzeichnis der Audios zum Hörverstehen
Hörverstehenstexte aus dem Workbook

Zusätzlich: Lesetexte des Schülerbuchs als MP3-Dateien

Die Hörtexte gibt es auch online als MP3-Dateien zum Herunterladen. Dazu den Code **fe76m3** ins Suchfeld auf www.klett.de eingeben.